THE KEFALONIA ADVENTURE: A TRAVEL PREPARATION GUIDE

SHONDA WILLIAMS

Table of Contents

Introduction

Kefalonia is a Greek island full of natural beauty, rich history, and charming culture. If you are looking for a relaxing beach holiday, an adventurous outdoor experience, or a cultural immersion, Kefalonia has something for you. In this travel guide, you will find everything you need to know to plan your perfect trip to Kefalonia.

Kefalonia is the largest and most diverse island in the Ionian Sea, with a coastline of over 250 km and a terrain that ranges from lush forests to rugged mountains. It is also home to the only national park on a Greek island, where you can hike up Mount Ainos and admire the rare fir trees and wild horses. Kefalonia's beaches are among the best in Greece, with crystal-clear waters and stunning scenery. Some of the most popular ones are Myrtos, Antisamos, Lourdas, Skala, and Xi. You can also visit the hidden coves and caves by hiring a boat or joining a tour.

Kefalonia's history dates back to ancient times when it was part of the kingdom of Odysseus, the legendary hero of Homer's epic poem. You can see the remains of ancient walls and temples when you visit the archaeological sites of Sami and Krani. You can also learn about the more recent history of Kefalonia, which was marked by Venetian rule, the Napoleonic wars, the World War II occupation, and the devastating earthquake of 1953. The island's culture and traditions have been shaped by these events, as well as by the influence of other Ionian islands and Italy. When you visit the picturesque villages of Fiskardo and Assos, which have preserved their original architecture and charm, you get to experience the local lifestyle of Kefalonia. You can also enjoy the delicious cuisine of Kefalonia, which is based on fresh seafood, meat, cheese, olive oil, and honey. Don't miss the chance to taste the local specialities, such as kreatopita (meat pie), riganada (bread with tomato and oregano), and robola (white wine).

Kefalonia is a destination that will surprise you with its diversity and beauty. It is an island that combines natural wonders, historical attractions, cultural heritage, and friendly people. It is an island that will make you fall in love with Greece. In this travel guide, you will find all the information you need to make your Kefalonia holidays unforgettable. Keep reading to discover more about Kefalonia's top attractions, beaches, hotels, restaurants, and things to do.

Chapter 1 • Welcome to Kefalonia

Why Visit Kefalonia?

Below are some of the reasons why you should visit Kefalonia:

Beaches: With crystal-clear waters and a serene atmosphere, Kefalonia has some of the most stunning beaches in Greece. Some of them include Myrtos, Antisamos, Lourdas, Skala, and Xi.

History and Culture: Kefalonia has a long and rich history that spans from ancient times to modern days. The Venetian fortresses of Assos and St George testify to the island's strategic importance in the Mediterranean. These events have shaped the island's character and identity, as well as its architecture and culture.

National Parks: Kefalonia is a great place for wildlife lovers, as you can spot sea turtles, dolphins, seals, and birds in their natural habitats.

Food: Kefalonia's local specialities include kreatopita (meat pie), riganada (bread with tomato and oregano), and robola (white wine).

Festivals and Celebrations: Some festivals and celebrations that take place throughout the year include Carnival, Easter, Saint Gerasimos Day, and Robola Wine Festival.

These are just some of the reasons why you should visit Kefalonia. If you want to discover more about this amazing island, keep reading this travel guide.

Chapter 2 • Planning Your Trip

Best Time to Visit Kefalonia

The best time to visit Kefalonia depends on what you are looking for in your holiday. Kefalonia has a Mediterranean climate with hot dry summers and mild winters. However, each season has its advantages and disadvantages, so here are some factors to consider when planning your trip:

Weather: If you want to enjoy the sun and the sea, the summer months of June to August are the ideal choice. The average temperature is around 30°C, the sunshine hours are between 11 and 12 per day, and the rainfall is minimal. The beaches are at their best, with clear blue waters and white sand or pebbles. You can also join various water sports and activities, such as sailing, kayaking, snorkelling, and diving. However, be aware that the summer is also the peak season for tourism, so expect higher prices, more crowds, and less availability for accommodation and transportation.

Crowd: If you prefer a more comfortable and quiet holiday, the spring and autumn months of April to May and September to October are good alternatives. The average temperature is around 20°C, the sunshine hours are between 7 and 10 per day, and the rainfall is moderate. The weather is still warm enough to enjoy the beaches, but not too hot to explore the island's attractions. You can also benefit from lower prices, fewer tourists, and more availability for hotels and flights. However, be prepared for some occasional showers and storms, especially on October 12.

Festivals and Celebrations: If you are interested in the island's history and culture, the winter months of November to March are a great opportunity to discover Kefalonia's heritage. The average temperature is around 10°C, the sunshine hours are between 4 and 6 per day, and the rainfall is high. The weather is mild and pleasant for visiting the archaeological sites, museums, churches, and monuments of Kefalonia. You can also experience the local festivals and celebrations, such as Carnival, Easter, Saint Gerasimos Day, and Robola Wine Festival. However, keep in mind that winter is also the low season for tourism, so many hotels, restaurants, and shops may be closed or have limited hours. You may also face some difficulties in finding direct flights from European cities to Kefalonia.

As you can see, Kefalonia is a wonderful island that can be visited all year round. However, depending on your preferences and expectations, some months may be more suitable than others. In this travel guide, you will find more information about Kefalonia's weather and seasons, as well as its top attractions, beaches, hotels, restaurants, and things to do. Keep reading to learn more about this amazing island.

Visa Requirements and Travel Documents

If you are planning to visit Kefalonia, you need to make sure you have the necessary visa requirements and travel documents for your trip. Depending on your nationality, the purpose and duration of your stay, and the countries you are travelling from or to, you may need to apply for a visa, a passport, or a national ID card. Below are some general guidelines to help you prepare for your journey:

Kefalonia is part of Greece, which is a member of the European Union (EU) and the Schengen Area. This means that if you are a citizen of another EU or Schengen country, you can travel to Kefalonia without a visa, as long as you have a valid passport or national ID card that shows your nationality. However, you should be prepared to show your travel documents at any time, as border controls may be restored at short notice.

If you are a citizen of a non-EU or non-Schengen country, you may need to apply for a visa to enter Kefalonia, depending on the visa policy of Greece and the Schengen Area. You can check if you need a visa and how to apply for one on the official website of the Greek Ministry of Foreign Affairs. You will also need a valid passport that is issued less than 10 years before the date of your entry and is valid for at least 3 months after the date of your departure. Some countries may also have special visa conditions and rules regarding the length of validity remaining on your passport. You should contact the relevant authorities (e.g. embassy or consulate) for further information.

If you are travelling to Kefalonia from or via the United Kingdom (UK), you should be aware that the UK has left the EU and is no longer part of the Schengen Area. This means that there may be changes in the entry requirements and travel documents for UK citizens and residents travelling to Kefalonia. You should check the latest travel advice from the UK government1 and the Greek government before your trip.

Regardless of your nationality, you should also make sure you have all the necessary travel documents organised well before your day of departure. You should have a valid ticket or flight reservation with your name matching your form of identification. You should also complete a Passenger Locator Form (PLF) at least 24 hours before you arrive in Greece, as this is mandatory for all travellers entering the country. You can find more information and fill in the PLF online on the official website of the Greek government.

In addition to the visa requirements and travel documents, you should also be aware of the public health requirements and safety measures related to the COVID-19 pandemic. Depending on your vaccination status, test results, and country of origin or transit, you may need to present a negative PCR test, an antigen test, a vaccination certificate, or a recovery certificate upon arrival in Greece. You may also need to undergo random testing or quarantine at your destination. You should check the latest updates and guidelines from the Greek government and the UK government1 (if applicable) before your trip.

Before you embark on your adventure, you need to make sure you have all the necessary visa requirements and travel documents for your trip. This will help you avoid any problems or delays at the border or during your stay.

Airports and Airlines

If you are travelling to Kefalonia by air, you will most likely arrive at Kefalonia International Airport, which is the only airport on the island. Kefalonia Airport is located in the southwest of the island, 8 km away from the capital Argostoli. The airport has a brand new terminal that opened in 2020, following the latest EU regulations and providing a seamless arrival and departure service for all international tourists visiting Kefalonia.

Kefalonia Airport is served by several airlines, both regular and charter, that connect the island with many destinations in Europe and beyond. Some of the main airlines that fly to and from Kefalonia Airport are:

Aegean Airlines: The largest Greek airline, offering flights to Athens and other Greek islands.

British Airways: The flag carrier of the United Kingdom, offering flights to London–Heathrow.

Condor: A German leisure airline, offering flights to Düsseldorf and Frankfurt.

EasyJet: A British low-cost airline, offering flights to Amsterdam, Bristol, Edinburgh, London–Gatwick, London–Luton, Manchester, Milan–Malpensa, and Naples.

Jet2: A British low-cost airline, offering flights to Birmingham, Bristol, East Midlands, Glasgow, Leeds/Bradford, London–Stansted, Manchester, and Newcastle upon Tyne.

Ryanair: An Irish low-cost airline, offering flights to Athens and other European cities.

Sky Express: A Greek regional airline, offering flights to Athens and other Greek islands.

TUI: A British travel company, offering flights to various European destinations.

Volotea: A Spanish low-cost airline, offering flights to Venice and other Italian cities.

You can find the full list of airlines and destinations on the official website of Kefalonia Airport. You can also compare prices and book your flights online using various travel websites or apps. However, be aware that some flights may be seasonal or subject to change due to the COVID-19 pandemic. You should always check the latest travel advice and updates from your airline and the Greek government before your trip.

Currency and Money Matters

One of the most important things to consider when travelling to Kefalonia is the currency and money matters. You need to know what kind of money you will need, how to exchange it, how to use it, and how to manage it during your stay. Below are some tips and information to help you with your financial planning:

The currency of Kefalonia is the Euro, which is the official currency of Greece and most of the European Union countries. The Euro is divided into 100 cents, and there are coins of 1, 2, 5, 10, 20, and 50 cents, as well as 1 and 2 Euros. There are also banknotes of 5, 10, 20, 50, 100, 200, and 500 Euros.

The best way to get Euros for your trip is to buy them before you leave your home country, as you will usually get a better exchange rate and avoid extra fees. You can order your Euros online or at your local bank or travel agency. You can also use a travel money card that allows you to load Euros onto it and use it like a debit card.

If you need more Euros during your stay in Kefalonia, you can withdraw them from ATMs or exchange them at banks or foreign exchange offices. However, be aware that some ATMs may charge a fee for withdrawals, and some banks or foreign exchange offices may offer a lower exchange rate or charge a commission. You should always compare the rates and fees before you make a transaction. You should also inform your bank or card provider that you are travelling to Kefalonia, as they may block your card if they suspect fraudulent activity.

When paying for goods or services in Kefalonia, you can use cash or a card, depending on the availability and preference of the seller. Most shops, restaurants, hotels, and other businesses accept credit or debit cards, but some may only accept cash or have a minimum amount for card payments. You should always ask before you pay and have some cash on hand for emergencies. You should also keep your receipts and check your statements regularly for any errors or unauthorized charges.

When tipping in Kefalonia, you can follow the local custom of rounding up the bill or leaving a small amount of change. Tipping is not mandatory, but it is appreciated as a sign of gratitude for good service. You can tip between 5% and 10% of the bill at restaurants, cafes, bars, and taxis. You can also tip a few Euros per day to hotel staff, tour guides, drivers, and other service providers.

Transportation in Kefalonia

To explore Kefalonia and enjoy its beauty, you need to know how to get around and what transportation options are available. Below are some tips and information to help you with your transportation in Kefalonia:

The most convenient and flexible way to move around Kefalonia is by car or motorbike. You can rent a vehicle from various agencies at the airport, ports, or towns, and drive to any destination on the island at your own pace. However, you should be careful when driving, as some roads are narrow, winding, or unpaved. You should also have a valid driver's license, insurance, and an international driving permit if required.

If you prefer public transportation, you can use the buses operated by KTEL Kefalonias, which connect the main towns and villages of the island. The buses are cheap, reliable, and frequent, but they may not cover all the areas or attractions you want to visit. The central bus station is located in Argostoli, but there are also stations in Sami, Poros, and Lixouri. You can check the timetables and routes on the official website of KTEL Kefalonias.

Another option for public transportation is the ferry boat that runs between Argostoli and Lixouri. The ferry is fast, cheap, and scenic, and it can save you time and distance if you want to travel between the two towns. The ferry operates every 30 minutes during the day and every hour during the night. You can buy your tickets at the port or on board.

If you want to travel by taxi or private transfer, you can find many taxis in Kefalonia, especially at the airport, ports, and towns. The taxis are comfortable and fast, but they can be expensive if you want to travel long distances. You can book a taxi by calling one of the numbers provided by various taxi services, or you can book a private transfer online using various travel websites or apps. You should always agree on the fare before you get in the taxi or transfer.

Accommodation Options

One of the most important aspects of planning your trip is choosing the right accommodation option for your needs and preferences. Kefalonia offers a wide range of accommodation options, from luxury hotels and villas to budget-friendly apartments and studios. Below are some of the main types of accommodation options you can find on the island:

Hotels: If you are looking for comfort, convenience, and service, hotels are a great choice for your stay in Kefalonia. You can find hotels of various categories and styles, from boutique and family-friendly to spa and beachfront. Hotels usually offer facilities such as swimming pools, restaurants, bars, gyms, and Wi-Fi. Some of the best-rated hotels in Kefalonia are Canale

Hotel & Suites, Electra Kefalonia Hotel & Spa, Petani Resort, and Kefalonia Bay Palace.

Villas: If you are looking for privacy, space, and luxury, villas are a perfect option for your stay in Kefalonia. You can rent a villa with your pool, garden, terrace, and kitchen, and enjoy the stunning views of the sea or the mountains. Villas are ideal for families, groups, or couples who want to have a home away from home. Some of the best-rated villas in Kefalonia are Villa Pilali, Sun N Sea Kefalonia Villa, Saint George Castle Villa with sea view, and Villa Estia Spartia Kefalonia.

Apartments: If you are looking for affordability, flexibility, and independence, apartments are a great option for your stay in Kefalonia. You can find apartments of various sizes and locations, from studios to penthouses. Apartments usually have a kitchenette or a fully equipped kitchen, a living room, a bathroom, and a balcony or patio. Apartments are ideal for solo travellers, couples, or small families who want to have more control over their budgets and schedules. Some of the best-rated apartments in Kefalonia are Mary's Studios & Apartment, Yialos Apartments, Lakithra Apartments, and Katarina Apartments.

These are just some of the main types of accommodation options you can find in Kefalonia. You can also find other options such as guesthouses, hostels, campsites, or bed and breakfasts. You can compare prices and book your accommodation online using various travel websites or apps.

Chapter 3 • Kefalonia Culture and Etiquette

Kefalonia Language and Basic Phrases

Before you embark on your adventure, you may want to learn some basic facts and phrases about the language of Kefalonia. Below are some tips and information to help you communicate with the locals and enjoy your stay:

The main language of Kefalonia is Greek, which is also the official language of Greece and one of the official languages of the European Union. Greek is a beautiful but complex language that has a different alphabet, grammar, and pronunciation from English. Greek has 24 letters, which are divided into vowels and consonants. Some letters look similar to English ones but have different sounds. For example, the letter H is pronounced as E, the letter P is pronounced as R, and the letter X is pronounced as KS.

Greek is also a highly inflected language, which means that the endings of words change according to their gender, number, case, tense, mood, and voice. For example, the word for "the" can be o (masculine singular nominative), I (feminine singular nominative), to (neuter singular nominative), oi (masculine plural nominative), tis (feminine plural nominative), or ta (neuter plural nominative), depending on the noun it modifies.

Greek has many dialects and variations, depending on the region, island, or village. Kefalonia has its dialect, which is influenced by the Venetian, Italian, and French languages. Some words or expressions may be different from standard Greek or other dialects. For example, in Kefalonia, they say "yia sou" for hello or goodbye, instead of "yia sas" or "yia mas". They also say "kala" for good or well, instead of "kali" or "kalo".

Despite the difficulty of learning Greek, you will find that most people in Kefalonia speak English, especially in tourist areas. English is widely taught in schools and used in business and media. Many locals also speak Italian, as Kefalonia has close ties with Italy. You will have no problem communicating with the locals in English or Italian.

However, it is always polite and appreciated to learn some basic phrases and words in Greek. The locals will be happy to hear you trying to speak their language and will help you if you make mistakes. Learning some Greek will also help you read signs, menus, and labels. Below are some useful phrases and words to get you started:

Hello - yia sou
Good morning - kalimera
Good afternoon - kalispera
Good night - kalinikta
Goodbye - adio
Yes - ne
No - ohi
Please - parakalo
Thank you - efharisto
Sorry - signomi
How are you? - Ti kaneis?
I'm fine, thank you - Kala, efharisto
What's your name? - Pos se lene?
My name is... - Me lene...
Where are you from? - Apo pou ise?

I'm from... - Ime apo...

Do you speak English? - Milas anglika?

I don't speak Greek - Den milao ellinika

I don't understand - Den katalaveno

Can you help me? - Boris na me voithisis?

Where is...? - Pou ine...?

How much is...? - Poso kani...?

Can I have...? - Boron a who...?

Cheers! - Yamas!

Delicious! - Nostimo!

Beautiful! - Oraio!

These are just some of the basic facts and phrases about the language of Kefalonia. You can practice your Greek with the locals or with other travellers. Learning some Greek will enrich your experience and make your trip more enjoyable.

Cultural Norms and Customs

Below are some of the main points to keep in mind:

Kefalonians are friendly, hospitable, and proud of their island and heritage. They will welcome you with warmth and generosity, and they will expect you to respect their customs and traditions. You should always greet them with a smile and a "yia sou" (hello), and thank them with an "efharisto" (thank you). You should also try to learn some basic phrases in Greek, as this will show your interest and appreciation for their language and culture.

Kefalonians are very social and expressive, and they like to talk, laugh, gesture, and hug. They may also touch your arm or shoulder during a conversation, or kiss you on both cheeks when meeting or parting. This is a sign of friendship and affection, and you should not be offended or uncomfortable by it. However, you should avoid any public displays of affection with your partner, as this may be considered inappropriate or disrespectful.

Kefalonians are very religious and devout, and they have many churches and monasteries on the island. You should always dress modestly and behave respectfully when visiting these places of worship. You should also remove your shoes, hats, or sunglasses, and cover your shoulders and knees. You should not take photos or videos without permission, or disturb the people who are praying or attending a service.

Kefalonians are very festive and celebratory, and they have many festivals and events throughout the year. You should join them in their celebrations and enjoy their music, dance, food, and wine. You should also participate in their customs and rituals, such as throwing flowers or breaking plates. However, you should not drink too much or cause any trouble, as this may be seen as rude or offensive.

Kefalonians are very relaxed and laid-back, and they have a different sense of time than most Westerners. They may not be very punctual or stick to a strict schedule. They may also take long breaks or siestas during the day, especially in the summer. You should not be impatient or annoyed by this but rather adapt to their pace and enjoy the moment.

Understanding and respecting the culture of Kefalonia will enrich your experience and make your trip more enjoyable.

Dining Etiquette

One of the most enjoyable aspects of travelling to Kefalonia is experiencing the delicious and diverse Greek cuisine. However, before you indulge in mouth-watering dishes and drinks, you may want to learn some basic facts and tips about the dining etiquette of Kefalonia. Below are some of the main points to keep in mind:

Dining in Kefalonia is a social and communal affair, and it is seen as an important opportunity to talk and be with family and friends. Greeks eat out a lot, especially in the evening and usually with a large group of people. At lunch, it is common for each person to have their own dish, but at dinner, all dishes go into the middle of the table for everyone to share. Everything is shared, and it is polite to offer food to others or put food on their plates without them asking.

Dining in Kefalonia is also a relaxed and laid-back affair, and it is not uncommon for meals to last for several hours. Greeks do not rush when eating but rather enjoy the food, the company, and the conversation. They may also take long breaks between courses or dishes, especially in the summer. You should not be impatient or annoyed by this but rather adapt to their pace and enjoy the moment.

Dining in Kefalonia is also a festive and celebratory affair, and it is often accompanied by music, dance, and wine. Greeks love to sing, clap, and dance along with the live music that is played in many restaurants and tavernas. They may also join in some customs and rituals, such as throwing flowers or breaking plates. You should not be shy or embarrassed by this but rather join them in their fun and joy.

When dining in Kefalonia, you should also be aware of some basic table manners and etiquette rules. Below are some of them:

You should always wait for the host or the guest of honour to start eating before you do. You should also follow their lead when finishing or leaving the table.

You should always use utensils when eating, except for some finger foods such as bread or souvlaki. You should not use your hands for other foods, as this may be considered rude or strange.

You should always eat everything on your plate, as this shows your appreciation for the food and the host. You should not leave any food behind, as this may be seen as wasteful or insulting.

You should always compliment the food and the cook, as this shows your gratitude and respect. You should not criticize or complain about the food, as this may be seen as rude or offensive.

You should always offer to pay for your share of the bill, as this shows your generosity and courtesy. You should not expect the host or anyone else to pay for you unless they insist or invite you explicitly.

You should always tip between 5% and 10% of the bill at restaurants, cafes, bars, and taxis. Tipping is not mandatory, but it is appreciated as a sign of gratitude for good service. You should also tip a few euros per day to hotel staff, tour guides, drivers, and other service providers.

Dress Code and Fashion in Kefalonia

Below are some of the main points to keep in mind:

Kefalonia has a Mediterranean climate with hot dry summers and mild winters. The average temperature is around 20°C, but it can vary depending on the season and the location. You should pack clothes that are suitable for the weather and the activities you plan to do. You should also bring a hat, sunglasses, sunscreen, and a jacket or sweater for the evenings or the mountains.

Kefalonia has a casual and relaxed dress code, and you can wear whatever you feel comfortable and confident in. You can wear shorts, t-shirts, dresses, skirts, jeans, or anything else that suits your style and personality. You can also wear bright colours, patterns, and accessories to express your individuality and creativity.

However, you should also be respectful of the local culture and traditions, and avoid wearing anything too revealing, provocative, or offensive. You should also dress modestly and appropriately when visiting places of worship, such as churches or monasteries. You should cover your shoulders and knees, and remove your shoes, hats, or sunglasses. You should not take photos or videos without permission, or disturb the people who are praying or attending a service.

Kefalonia has a vibrant fashion scene, and you can find many shops, boutiques, markets, and designers that offer a variety of clothes and accessories. You can find anything from traditional Greek costumes and handicrafts to modern and trendy outfits and jewellery. You can also find some local brands and products that are unique to Kefalonia, such as leather goods, embroidery, lace, pottery, honey, olive oil, and wine.

Kefalonia has some hotels and restaurants that have a more formal dress code, especially for dinner. You may need to wear long trousers and covered shoes for men, and dresses or skirts for women. You may also need to make a reservation in advance or follow some etiquette rules. You should always check the dress code and the requirements before you go to these places.

Festivals and Celebrations

Below are some of the most important and popular ones: **Carnival**: Carnival is a festive season that precedes Lent, the 40 days of fasting and repentance before Easter. Carnival is celebrated in Kefalonia with colourful parades, costumes, masks, music, dance, and fun. The most famous carnival events are held in Argostoli and Lixouri, where the "Kavalieri" (men dressed in white skirts) and their "Dames" (women dressed in elegant gowns) dance the traditional dances of Kefalonia. There are also contests, games, parties, and fireworks.

Easter: Easter is the most important religious festival for the Greeks, who commemorate the death and resurrection of Jesus Christ. Easter is celebrated in Kefalonia with solemn ceremonies, processions, rituals, and customs. On Good Friday, the Epitaphios (a wooden bier decorated with flowers that represent the tomb of Christ) are carried around the streets by the faithful. On Easter Sunday, people gather to roast lamb on the spit and crack red eggs (symbolizing the blood and life of Christ). On Easter Monday, there is a procession of the icon of Sissia Monastery in Vlachata.

Robola Wine Festival: Robola is a white wine produced in Kefalonia from a local grape variety. The Robola Wine Festival is held every year on the third weekend of August in two villages: Fragata and Valsamata. The festival is organized by the Cooperation of Robiola Producers in Kefalonia and lasts two days. The festival offers free robola wine, food, music, dance, and entertainment to thousands of visitors.

Feast of Agios Gerasimos: Agios Gerasimos is the patron saint of Kefalonia, who lived as a monk on the island in the 16th century. He is revered for his miracles and his relics are kept in a monastery that bears his name. The feast of Agios Gerasimos is held twice a year: on August 16th and October 20th. On these days, thousands of pilgrims flock to the monastery to venerate the saint's relics and attend the holy mass. There are also festivities with food, music, dance, and stalls.

Saristra Festival: Saristra Festival is a modern cultural event that takes place every summer in Sami. The festival showcases various forms of art, such as music, theatre, cinema, photography, painting, and literature. The festival is held in the main square of Sami (named Saristra) and in some half-ruined mansions that serve as exhibition spaces. The festival attracts many talented artists and visitors who want to enjoy a unique artistic experience.

Chapter 4 • Exploring Kefalonia

Top Attractions

Myrtos Beach

One of the most spectacular and famous beaches in Kefalonia is Myrtos Beach, located in the northwest of the island, about 29 km from Argostoli. Myrtos Beach is a stunning sight that will take your breath away with its white pebbles, turquoise waters, and dramatic cliffs. It is no wonder that Myrtos Beach has been voted several times as one of the best beaches in the world by various travel magazines.

Myrtos Beach has a semi-circular shape that stretches for about one kilometre along the coast. The beach is surrounded by tall marble cliffs that create a contrast with the blue sea and the green vegetation. The beach is accessible by a steep and winding road that offers amazing views of the bay. You can also admire the sunset from the road, as it creates a beautiful palette of colours on the water and the sky.

Myrtos Beach is well-organized with sunbeds, umbrellas, changing rooms, toilets, and a snack bar. However, there is also enough space for those who prefer to enjoy the beach more naturally. The beach is ideal for swimming, sunbathing, and relaxing, but you should be careful of the waves and the currents, especially when it is windy. The water is very clear and deep, but it can also be cold sometimes.

Myrtos Beach is not only a place for relaxation but also for adventure and fun. You can join various water sports and activities, such as sailing, kayaking, snorkelling, and diving. You can also explore the hidden caves and coves that are located along the coast. You can also hike up to the cliffs and enjoy the panoramic views of the beach and the sea.

Myrtos Beach is a must-see attraction for anyone who visits Kefalonia. It is a beach that will impress you with its beauty and charm. It is a beach that will make you fall in love with Kefalonia.

Melissani Cave

Melissani Cave is one of the most impressive and beautiful attractions in Kefalonia and a must-see for anyone who visits the island. It is a natural wonder that will amaze you with its crystal-clear waters, its stunning rock formations, and its magical atmosphere.

Melissani Cave is located near the village of Karavomylos, about 5 km southeast of Agia Effimia and 29 km from Argostoli. It is a lake cave that was formed by the erosion of limestone rocks over millions of years. The cave has two chambers, separated by an island in the middle. The first chamber is open to the sky, as the roof collapsed centuries ago, creating a large hole that lets the sunlight in. The second chamber is dark and full of stalactites and stalagmites that have different shapes and colours.

The best way to explore Melissani Cave is by taking a boat tour that lasts about 15 minutes. You can enter the cave through an underground tunnel and then board a small wooden boat that will take you around the lake. You will be able to admire the beauty of the cave from different angles and perspectives, as well as learn some interesting facts and stories from your guide. The highlight of the tour is when you reach the open chamber, where the sun's rays reflect on the water and create a dazzling effect of blue light. The water is so clear that you can see the bottom of the lake, which is about 20 to 30 meters deep.

Melissani Cave is not only a natural attraction, but also a place of myth and legend. According to Greek mythology, the cave was named after Melissanthi, a nymph who fell in love with Pan, the god of nature and music. However, Pan did not return her feelings, so she threw herself into the lake and died. Her name means "honey bee" in Greek, and some people believe that her spirit still haunts the cave. Archaeological excavations in 1962 revealed many artefacts from the 3rd and 4th century BC, such as pottery, coins, and figurines of nymphs, which confirm the ancient worship of Melissanthi and Pan in the cave.

Fiskardo

Fiskardo is a charming and picturesque village on the northern tip of Kefalonia, the largest of the Ionian islands. Fiskardo is one of the few places in Kefalonia that survived the devastating earthquake of 1953, which preserved its original Venetian architecture and atmosphere. Fiskardo is a popular destination for tourists and yachtsmen, who come to enjoy its natural beauty, its rich history, and its lively nightlife.

Fiskardo has a beautiful harbour that is filled with colourful boats, cafes, restaurants, and shops. You can stroll along the waterfront and admire the views of the sea and the nearby island of Ithaca. You can also visit the 18th-century lighthouse and the Byzantine basilica that is located at the entrance of the harbor. Fiskardo has a museum that displays various artefacts and exhibits related to the history and culture of the village.

Fiskardo is surrounded by stunning beaches, coves, and forests that offer many opportunities for swimming, sunbathing, hiking, and exploring. Some of the most popular beaches near Fiskardo are Emblisi, Dafnoudi, Alaties, and Agia Jerusalem. You can also take a boat trip to discover the hidden gems of the coast, such as Foki Bay, Assos Village, or Myrtos Beach.

Fiskardo is also a great place to experience the local cuisine, which is based on fresh seafood, meat, cheese, olive oil, and honey. You can taste some of the specialities of Kefalonia, such as kreatopita (meat pie), riganada (bread with tomato and oregano), and robola (white wine). You can also join some of the festivals and celebrations that take place in Fiskardo throughout the year, such as Carnival, Easter, Robola Wine Festival, and Feast of Agios Gerasimos.

Mount Ainos National Park

Mount Ainos National Park is the only national park situated on a Greek island, and it covers an area of about 3,000 hectares on the highest mountain range of the Ionian Islands.

Mount Ainos National Park is famous for its unique fir tree forest, which is dominated by the endemic species of Abies cephalonica. This rare and majestic tree grows up to 35 meters high and has needle-like leaves that create a dense canopy. The forest covers two-thirds of the park's area and creates a contrast between the blue sea and the green vegetation. The forest is home to many animals and plants, some of which are endangered or protected, such as wild horses, golden eagles, orchids, and mushrooms.

Mount Ainos National Park offers many opportunities for hiking, biking, camping, and exploring. Five marked trails vary in length and difficulty, from easy to moderate. You can choose the trail that suits your preferences and abilities, and enjoy the stunning views of the island and the sea. The most popular trail is the one that leads to the summit of Megas Soros, which is 1,628 meters high and offers a panoramic view of the

Ionian Sea, the Peloponnese, and the neighbouring islands. You can also visit some of the caves that are located along the trails, such as Petasi and Nyfi.

Mount Ainos National Park is not only a natural attraction, but also a place of history and culture. According to Greek mythology, the mountain was named after Ainos, a son of Zeus and Protogeneia. The mountain was also a refuge for the rebels during the Greek War of Independence in 1821. The park has a museum that displays various artefacts and exhibits related to the history and culture of the mountain and the island.

Other Attractions

Below are some of the other attractions that you can explore and enjoy on the island:

Antisamos Beach: Antisamos Beach is one of the most beautiful and popular beaches in Kefalonia, located on the east coast, near the town of Sami. It is a pebble beach with crystal-clear waters and green hills that create stunning scenery. The beach is well-organized with sunbeds, umbrellas, showers, and a beach bar. It is also ideal for water sports, such as kayaking, snorkelling, and diving.

Agios Gerasimos Monastery: Agios Gerasimos Monastery is one of the most important religious sites in Kefalonia, located in the Omala Valley, near the village of Valsamata. It is dedicated to Saint Gerasimos, the patron saint of Kefalonia, who lived as a monk on the island in the 16th century. He is revered for his miracles and his relics are kept in a silver casket in the monastery. The monastery has a beautiful church with frescoes and icons, a museum with religious artefacts, and a garden with a plane tree under which Saint Gerasimos used to pray.

Fiscardo Lighthouse: Fiscardo Lighthouse is a charming attraction on the northern tip of Kefalonia, near the village of Fiscardo. It is an 18th-century lighthouse that was rebuilt after the earthquake of 1953. It has a white tower and a red dome that stands out against the blue sea and the green landscape. The lighthouse offers a panoramic view of the Ionian Sea, the island of Ithaca, and the mainland. It is also a romantic spot to watch the sunset.

Korgialenio Historical and Folklore Museum: The Korgialenio Historical and Folklore Museum is a cultural attraction in Argostoli, the capital of Kefalonia. It is housed in a neoclassical building that was donated by Marinos Korgialenios, a benefactor of Kefalonia. The museum displays various exhibits and collections related to the history and culture of Kefalonia, such as costumes, jewellery, tools, weapons, coins, paintings, photographs, and documents.

Skala Beach: Skala Beach is one of the longest and most popular beaches in Kefalonia, located on the south coast, near the village of Skala. It is a sandy beach with clear waters and pine trees that provide shade and freshness. The beach is well-organized with sunbeds, umbrellas, showers, and water sports facilities. It is also ideal for families with children, as it has shallow waters and a playground. Near the beach, you can find many hotels, restaurants, bars, and shops.

Best Beaches

Antisamos: Antisamos Beach is one of the most beautiful and popular beaches on Kefalonia, the largest of the Ionian islands. It is located on the east coast, near the port of Sami, and about 30 km from the capital Argostoli. Antisamos Beach is famous for its natural beauty, which consists of turquoise waters, white pebbles, and green hills that create stunning scenery. It is also famous for being one of the locations for the Hollywood movie "Captain Corelli's Mandolin", which was filmed on the island in 2001.

Lourdas: Lourdas Beach is well-organized with sunbeds, umbrellas, changing rooms, toilets, and a snack bar. However, there is also enough space for those who prefer to enjoy the beach more naturally. The beach is ideal for swimming, sunbathing, and relaxing, but you should be careful of the waves and the currents, especially when it is windy. The water is very clear and deep, but it can also be cold sometimes.

Skala: Skala Beach is a place for adventure and fun. You can join various water sports and activities, such as sailing, kayaking, snorkelling, and diving. You can also explore the hidden caves and coves that are located along the coast. You can also hike up to the cliffs and enjoy the panoramic views of the beach and the sea.

Petani: Petani Beach is located on the west coast, on the Paliki peninsula, near the town of Lixouri. Petani Beach is famous for its natural beauty, which consists of turquoise waters, white pebbles, and green hills that create stunning scenery.

Foki Beach: Foki Beach is a small and secluded beach near the village of Fiscardo, on the northern tip of

Kefalonia. It is named after the Mediterranean monk seals (fokia in Greek) that sometimes visit the bay. The beach has large pebbles and crystal-clear waters, surrounded by olive trees and cypresses. The beach is not organized, but there is a tavern nearby where you can have a meal or a drink.

Emblisi Beach: Emblisi Beach is another beautiful beach near Fiscardo, on the northern coast of Kefalonia. It is a pebble beach with turquoise waters and green hills that create stunning scenery. The beach is partly organized with sunbeds and umbrellas, but there is also enough space for those who prefer to enjoy the beach more naturally. The beach is ideal for swimming, sunbathing, and relaxing.

Dafnoudi Beach: Dafnoudi Beach is a hidden gem on the northern coast of Kefalonia, near the village of Antipata. It is a small and secluded beach with white pebbles and clear waters, surrounded by rocks and pine trees. The beach is not organized, but there is natural shade from the trees. To reach the beach, you have to walk for about 20 minutes through a forest path, but the reward is worth it.

Xi Beach: Xi Beach is one of the most unique and popular beaches on Kefalonia, located on the south coast, on the Paliki peninsula, near the town of Lixouri. It is famous for its red sand and clay, which give it a distinctive colour and texture. The beach is well-organized with sunbeds, umbrellas, showers, and water sports facilities. It is also ideal for families with children, as it has shallow waters and a playground. Near the beach, you can find many hotels, restaurants, bars, and shops.

Best Villages

Argostoli

Argostoli is the capital and largest town of Kefalonia, the largest of the Ionian Islands in Greece. It is a charming seaside town that offers a variety of attractions, activities, and experiences for visitors who want to explore the beauty and culture of this island. Below are some of the things you can do and see in Argostoli:

Visit the Archaeological Museum of Argostoli, which displays artefacts from the ancient and Roman periods of Kefalonia, such as pottery, coins, sculptures, and mosaics.

Walk across the De Bosset Bridge, the longest stone bridge in Europe, which was built by the British in the 19th century to connect Argostoli with the opposite shore of the Koutavos Lagoon. You can enjoy the views of the lagoon, which is a nature reserve and a habitat for the endangered loggerhead turtles.

Explore the Katavothres, a unique geological phenomenon where seawater enters sinkholes on the coast and reappears on the other side of the island after passing through underground channels. You can also see a watermill that was powered by this water flow.

Relax at one of the many beaches near Argostoli, such as Makris Gialos, Platis Gialos, Mediteranee, or Fanari, which offer clear blue waters, golden sand, and various facilities and services.

Enjoy the nightlife and entertainment options in Argostoli, which has many bars, clubs, cafes, and restaurants to suit every taste and mood. You can also catch a show at the Kefalos Theatre, which hosts cultural events and performances throughout year

Discover the history and architecture of Argostoli by visiting some of its landmarks, such as the Bell Tower, the Saint Spyridon Church, the Napier Garden, and the Vallianos Square. You can also admire some of the old mansions that survived the devastating earthquake of 1953, which destroyed most of the town.

Argostoli is a town that combines tradition and modernity, nature and culture, fun and relaxation. It is a great destination for anyone who wants to experience the full range of what Kefalonia has to offer.

Sami

Sami is a coastal town on the east coast of Kefalonia. It is a lively and attractive place that has a lot to offer to visitors who want to enjoy the natural beauty, cultural heritage, and gastronomic delights of this island. Below are some of the highlights of Sami:

Explore the ancient ruins of Sami, which was once a powerful and prosperous city-state in the classical era. It was mentioned by Homer in his epics and was involved in wars with Athens and Rome. You can see the remains of the Acropolis, the walls, the fortifications, and the theatre that testify to its glorious past.

Visit the museums of Sami, which showcase the rich history and maritime tradition of this town. The Archaeological Museum displays artefacts from prehistoric to Roman times, such as pottery, coins, sculptures, and mosaics. The Nautical Museum exhibits models of wooden ships that span 3,500 years of naval history, from ancient triremes to modern yachts.

Experience the wonders of nature in Sami, which is surrounded by lush greenery and stunning beaches. You can admire the unique phenomenon of Katavothres, where seawater enters sinkholes on the coast and reappears on the other side of the island through underground channels. You can also visit the amazing caves of Melissani and Drogarati, which are filled with stalactites, stalagmites, and crystal-clear water.

Relax at one of the many beaches near Sami, which offers clear blue waters, golden sand, and various facilities and services. Some of the most popular ones are Antisamos, Karavomylos, Agia Paraskevi, and Agia Efimia. You can also enjoy water sports, boat trips, fishing, or diving in the turquoise sea.

Enjoy the gastronomy and nightlife of Sami, which has many bars, cafes, restaurants, and taverns to suit every taste and mood. You can sample local delicacies such as robola wine, kreatopita (meat pie), aliada (garlic sauce), and mandola (almond sweets). You can also watch cultural events and performances at the Kefalos Theater or join the local festivals and celebrations.

Agia Efimia

Agia Efimia is a lovely fishing village on the east coast of Kefalonia. It is a great place to enjoy the scenic views, the local cuisine, and the friendly atmosphere of this island. Below are some of the reasons why you should visit Agia Efimia:

Agia Efimia has a small but charming harbour that faces the island of Ithaca, the legendary home of Odysseus. You can see many fishing boats and yachts moored there, or you can rent your boat and explore the coast at your own pace. You can also join a boat tour that will take you to the nearby islands or caves.

Agia Efimia has several museums that showcase the rich history and culture of this town and Kefalonia in general. You can visit the Archaeological Museum, which displays artefacts from different periods of Kefalonia's history, such as pottery, coins, sculptures, and mosaics. You can also visit the Nautical Museum, which exhibits models of wooden ships that span 3,500 years of naval history, from ancient triremes to modern yachts.

Agia Efimia is surrounded by nature and has some beautiful beaches to relax and swim. You can admire the phenomenon of Katavothres, where seawater enters sinkholes on the coast and reappears on the other side of the island through underground channels. You can also visit the caves of Melissani and Drogarati, which are filled with stalactites, stalagmites, and crystal-clear water. Some of the most popular beaches near Agia Efimia are Antisamos, Karavomylos, Agia Paraskevi, and Agia Efimia itself.

Agia Efimia has a variety of tavernas, bars, and restaurants that offer delicious local food and drinks. You can taste some of the specialities of Kefalonia, such as robola wine, kreatopita (meat pie), aliada (garlic sauce), and mandola (almond sweets). You can also enjoy the nightlife and entertainment options in Agia Efimia, which include live music, Greek dancing, cultural events, and festivals.

Lixouri

Lixouri is a beautiful and lively town on the west coast of Kefalonia. It is the main town of the Paliki peninsula and the second largest town on the island after Argostoli. Lixouri has a lot to offer to visitors who want to enjoy the scenic views, the local culture, and the friendly atmosphere of this island. Below are some of the things you can do and see in Lixouri:

Learn about the history and culture of Lixouri and Kefalonia at the museums and landmarks of the town. You can visit the Archaeological Museum, which displays artefacts from different periods of Kefalonia's history, such as pottery, coins, sculptures, and mosaics. You can also visit the Nautical Museum, which exhibits models of wooden ships that span 3,500 years of naval history, from ancient triremes to modern yachts. You can also admire some of the old churches, such as the Saint Spyridon Church, and some of the neoclassical buildings and mansions that survived the devastating earthquake of 1953.

Enjoy the natural beauty and diversity of Lixouri and its surroundings. You can explore the phenomenon of Katavothres, where seawater enters sinkholes on the coast and reappears on the other side of the island through underground channels. You can also visit the caves of Melissani and Drogarati, which are filled with stalactites, stalagmites, and crystal-clear water. You can also relax at one of the many beaches near Lixouri, such as Lepeda, Xi, Mega Lakos, or Petani, which offer clear blue waters, golden sand, and various facilities and services.

Experience the gastronomy and nightlife of Lixouri, which has a variety of tavernas, bars, and restaurants that offer delicious local food and drinks. You can taste some of the specialities of Kefalonia, such as robola wine, kreatopita (meat pie), aliada (garlic sauce), and mandola (almond sweets). You can also enjoy the nightlife and entertainment options in Lixouri, which include live music, Greek dancing, cultural events, and festivals.

Take a boat trip to the nearby islands or caves. You can rent your boat or join a boat tour that will take you to the island of Ithaca, the legendary home of Odysseus, or other islands such as Zakynthos or Lefkada. You can also visit some of the hidden caves along the coast, such as Fteri or Agios Gerasimos.

Other villages

Other than the main towns and villages of Kefalonia, many other smaller and less-known villages are worth visiting for their charm, beauty, and authenticity. Below are some of them:

Poros: Poros is a scenic town on the east coast of Kefalonia. It is a working port that connects Kefalonia with mainland Greece and other islands. It has a population of about 1100 inhabitants and a traditional Greek feel.

Karavados: This is a traditional village on the southern side of the island, in the area of Leivathos. It has stone houses, narrow alleys, and a lovely church dedicated to Saint Gerasimos, the patron saint of Kefalonia. It is also close to some beautiful beaches, such as Trapezaki and Lourdas.

Spartia: This is another picturesque village in the area of Leivathos, on the southeastern side of the island. It is built on a hillside and overlooks the Ionian Sea and the island of Zakynthos. It has a small port, a pebbly beach, and a few taverns and shops.

Zola: This is a secluded village on the western side of the island, in the area of Pylaros. It is surrounded by lush greenery and has a small bay with crystal-clear water. It is ideal for those who seek peace and tranquillity.

Old Vlachata: This is an abandoned village on the Paliki peninsula, on the western side of the island. It was destroyed by the earthquake of 1953 and its inhabitants moved to a new location nearby. However, some of the old houses have been restored and turned into guesthouses or museums. You can visit this village and get a glimpse of how life used to be in Kefalonia before the disaster.

These are just some examples of the many other villages that you can explore in Kefalonia. Each one has its character, history, and charm. You will surely find something that suits your taste and interests.

Chapter 5 • Kefalonia Cuisine and Food Experiences

Introduction to Kefalonia Cuisine

Kefalonian food is a blend of Greek, Italian, French, and British influences, using local ingredients and traditional recipes to create dishes that are unique and delicious. Below are some of the highlights of Kefalonia's cuisine that you should not miss when you visit this beautiful island.

Pies: Kefalonia is famous for its pies, which are made with hand-kneaded, flaky dough and various fillings. The most popular one is the meat pie, which contains a mixture of three types of meat (pork, goat, and beef), cooked with herbs, garlic, tomato paste, and Robola wine. Another speciality is the artichoke pie, which is made with fresh artichokes, eggs, cheese, and mint.

Other pies include the cod pie, the octopus pie, and the cheese pie.

Wild greens: Kefalonia has a variety of wild greens that grow on the island, such as leeks, poppies, cauliflowers, zucchini, porridge, flours, spinach, celery, and fennel. These greens are used to make salads, soups, or stews, or are cooked with eggs and cheese to make a dish called strapatsada. Wild greens are rich in vitamins and minerals and have a distinctive flavour.

Meat: Kefalonia's meat dishes are mainly based on goat meat, which is tender and lean. Goat is roasted in the oven with potatoes and herbs, or cooked in a clay pot with tomatoes and cheese. Another delicacy is the tsigaridia, which is goat meat stewed with wild garlic. Pork and beef are also used to make sausages, meatballs, or souvlaki (skewers).

Seafood: Kefalonia's seafood is fresh and abundant, thanks to its long coastline and fishing tradition. You can find fish such as sea bream, sea bass, red mullet, swordfish, tuna, anchovies, sardines, and mackerel, grilled or fried with lemon and olive oil. You can also enjoy shellfish such as mussels, clams, oysters, scallops, and shrimp, cooked in wine or tomato sauce. A special treat is the aliada (garlic sauce), which is served with salted cod or fried fish.

Cheese: Kefalonia produces some of the finest cheeses in Greece, such as feta (white cheese), kefalotyri (hard yellow cheese), ladotyri (oil cheese), myzithra (fresh cheese), and graviera (sweet cheese). These cheeses are used to make pies or salads or are eaten as appetizers with bread and wine. A local speciality is the mantoles (almond sweets), which are made with almonds, sugar, and graviera cheese.

Wine: Kefalonia has a long history of wine-making dating back to ancient times. The island's climate and soil are ideal for growing grapes such as Robola (white), Mavrodaphne (red), Moscato (white), Muscat (white), and Zakynthino (red). These wines are aromatic and fruity and pair well with the local cuisine. You can visit some of the wineries on the island to taste their products and learn more about their production process.

Kefalonia's cuisine is a feast for the senses that will make you fall in love with this island even more. Whether you prefer pies or seafood, meat or cheese, wine or sweets, you will find something to satisfy your appetite and delight your palate. Bon appétit!

Famous Kefalonia Dishes

Kefalonia is a paradise for food lovers, as it offers a variety of regional specialities that showcase the island's rich gastronomic heritage. Below are some of the regional specialities that you should not miss when you visit Kefalonia:

Riganada: This is a simple but tasty dish that consists of toasted bread slices topped with olive oil, oregano, salt, and feta cheese. It is often served as a snack or appetizer, accompanied by olives, tomatoes, and wine. Riganada is considered the traditional bread of Kefalonia, as it was made by the shepherds who used to dry their bread in the sun and season it with herbs and cheese.

Bourdeto: This is a spicy fish stew that is made with scorpion fish, tomato sauce, onion, garlic, vinegar, and red pepper flakes. It is one of the most popular dishes of Kefalonia, especially in the town of Fiskardo, where it originated. Bourdeto is usually served with boiled potatoes or rice and a glass of Robola wine.

Aliada: This is a garlic sauce that is served with salted cod or fried fish. It is made with mashed potatoes, garlic, olive oil, lemon juice, and parsley. Aliada is a typical

Lenten dish that is enjoyed by locals and visitors alike. It has a strong flavour and aroma that complement the fish perfectly.

Kreatopita: This is a meat pie that is made with three types of meat (pork, goat, and beef), cooked with herbs, garlic, tomato paste, and Robola wine. The filling is wrapped in hand-kneaded, flaky dough and baked in the oven until golden. Kreatopita is a hearty and delicious dish that can be eaten as a main course or as a snack.

Mantoles: These are almond sweets that are made with almonds, sugar, and graviera cheese. They are shaped into small balls and coated with powdered sugar. Mantoles are a traditional dessert of Kefalonia that are often offered as a gift or served at weddings and celebrations. They have a crunchy texture and a sweet and nutty flavour.

Famous Kefalonia Drinks

Kefalonia is a great place to enjoy a drink, whether you prefer wine, beer, spirits, or soft drinks. The island has a long tradition of producing and consuming beverages that reflect its culture and geography. Below are some of the famous Kefalonia drinks that you should try when you visit this island:

Robola: This is the most famous wine of Kefalonia, made from a white grape variety that grows on the slopes of Mt Ainos. Robola is a dry and crisp wine with a fruity and floral aroma and a refreshing acidity. It pairs well with seafood, cheese, and salads. You can visit some of the wineries on the island to taste Robola and other local wines, such as Mavrodaphne (a sweet red wine), Moscato (a sparkling white wine), and Zakynthino (a light red wine).

Ouzo: This is the national drink of Greece, a clear anise-flavoured spirit that turns milky when mixed with water or ice. Ouzo is usually served as an aperitif or with meze (small dishes) such as cheese, olives, and seafood. Ouzo is very popular in Kefalonia, where it is often drunk with meals or as a social drink. You can find ouzo in most tavernas and bars on the island.

Retsina: This is a type of wine that is flavoured with pine resin, giving it a distinctive taste and aroma. Retsina is an ancient drink that dates back to the time of the ancient Greeks, who used resin to seal the wine amphorae and preserve the wine from oxidation. Retsina is usually a white or rosé wine that is served chilled with food or as a refreshing drink. Some people love it, some people hate it, but you should try it at least once when you are in Kefalonia.

Mythos: This is a Greek beer that has become more and more popular in recent years, competing with the Dutch beers Heineken and Amstel that used to dominate the market. Mythos is a pale lager with a smooth and malty flavour and a moderate bitterness. It is ideal for hot summer days and goes well with grilled meat, fish, or cheese. You can find Mythos in most tavernas and supermarkets on the island.

Kefalonia's drinks are diverse and delicious, offering something for every taste and occasion. Whether you prefer wine or beer, ouzo or retsina, coffee or tea, you will find something to quench your thirst and delight your palate. Cheers!

Wine and Food Pairing

One of the pleasures of travelling to Kefalonia is enjoying its cuisine and wine, which are both rich and diverse. Kefalonia produces some of the finest wines in Greece, such as Robola, Mavrodaphne, Moscato, and Zakynthino. These wines are aromatic and fruity and pair well with the local dishes, which are influenced by Greek, Italian, French, and British cuisines. Below are some tips for pairing wine and food in Kefalonia:

Robola: It pairs well with seafood, cheese, and salads. Try it with the famous bourdeto. Robola is also a great match for the artichoke pie, which is made with fresh artichokes, eggs, cheese, and mint.

Mavrodaphne: This is a sweet red wine with a dark colour and a rich flavour of dried fruits, chocolate, and spices. It pairs well with desserts, cheese, and nuts. Try it with the mantoles. Mavrodaphne is also a good choice for the kreatopita, a meat pie that is made with three types of meat (pork, goat, and beef).

Moscato: This is a sparkling white wine with a low alcohol content and a sweet taste of honey, peach, and citrus. It pairs well with fruits, cakes, and pastries. Try it with the baklava, a pastry made with layers of filo dough filled with chopped nuts and soaked in honey syrup. Moscato is also a nice accompaniment for the riganada.

Zakynthino: This is a light red wine with a ruby colour and a fruity aroma of cherry, raspberry, and plum. It pairs well with grilled meat, cheese, and pizza. Try it with the souvlaki, skewers of marinated meat (usually pork or chicken) grilled over charcoal. Zakynthino is also a good partner for the tsigaridia, which is goat meat stewed with wild garlic.

Must-Visit Kefalonia Restaurants

Below are some of the must-visit Kefalonia restaurants that you should try when you visit this island:

Robolis: This is a family-run restaurant that specializes in traditional Kefalonian cuisine, using fresh and local ingredients. The restaurant is located in the village of Poulata, near the Melissani Cave. The menu features dishes such as kreatopita (meat pie), riganada (bread with cheese and oregano), tsigaridia (goat stew), and mantoles (almond sweets). The restaurant also has a wine cellar where you can taste Robola and other local wines.

Kallithea: This is a modern and elegant restaurant that offers a fusion of Mediterranean and international cuisine, with a focus on seafood. The restaurant is located on the main road between Argostoli and Sami. The menu features dishes such as grilled octopus, lobster pasta, salmon tartare, and lamb chops. The restaurant also has a bar where you can enjoy cocktails and live music.

Kastro Cafe: This is a cosy and charming cafe that serves breakfast, lunch, and dinner, with a view of the castle of St George. The cafe is located in the village of Peratata, near the capital of Argostoli. The menu features dishes such as omelettes, pancakes, sandwiches, salads, and burgers. The cafe also serves homemade cakes, pies, and ice cream.

Olive Lounge Restaurant and Bar: This is a stylish and romantic restaurant that offers a fine dining experience, with a view of the sea. The restaurant is located in the village of Lourdata, near the beach of Lourdas. The menu features dishes such as scallops, risotto, duck breast, and beef fillet. The restaurant also has a wine list that includes Robola and other Greek wines.

Vardiani Island Restaurant: This is a unique and scenic restaurant that is located on a small island near the village of Xi. The restaurant can be reached by boat or by swimming from the mainland. The menu features dishes such as seabream, mussels, shrimp saganaki, and chicken souvlaki. The restaurant also has a beach bar where you can enjoy drinks and snacks.

Culinary Experiences and Cooking Classes

Below are some of the options that you can choose from:

Viva Your Chef: This is a service that offers private cooking classes or local home-cooking meals at your accommodation. You can learn how to prepare authentic Kefalonian dishes such as meat pie, riganada, tsigaridia, and mantoles, using fresh and local ingredients. You can also taste Robola and other local wines from their wine cellar.

Taste Kefalonia Food Experience at Sea Rock ws: This is a restaurant that offers cooking classes in a beautiful setting overlooking the sea. You can learn how to make Greek appetizers like tzatziki and Kefalonian riganada, as well as your phyllo pie with meat or cheese. You can also enjoy a lunch with the dishes you have prepared, along with wine and dessert.

Chez Vassiliki: This is a cosy and charming cafe that offers cooking classes in the village of Peratata, near the castle of St George. You can learn how to make traditional Kefalonian sweets such as baklava, loukoumades, and pasteli, using honey, nuts, and sesame seeds. You can also taste homemade cakes, pies, and ice cream.

Kefalonia Tours: This is a tour company that offers cultural and historical tours around the island, as well as cooking classes in different locations. You can learn how to make dishes such as seafood saganaki, stuffed tomatoes, and moussaka, using fresh and organic ingredients. You can also visit wineries, olive groves, and honey farms.

Katia Stefanatou: This is a professional chef and food blogger who offers cooking classes in her home kitchen in Argostoli. You can learn how to make dishes such as spinach pie, lamb kleftiko, and yoghurt cake, using seasonal and local products. You can also get tips and tricks on how to improve your cooking skills.

Chapter 6 • Outdoor Activities and Nature

Hiking and Trekking in Kefalonia

Kefalonia is a perfect island for hiking and trekking enthusiasts, as it offers a variety of trails and routes. Below are some of the best hiking and trekking options in Kefalonia that you should consider for your travel guide:

Mount Ainos National Park: This is the most popular hiking destination in Kefalonia, as it is home to the highest peak of the Ionian Islands, Mount Ainos (or Mount Aenos), which stands at 1,628 m above sea level. The park is also a protected area for its unique flora and fauna, especially the endemic Kefalonian fir trees and the semi-wild horses that roam the slopes. Several trails lead to the summit or along the ridge of Mount Ainos, offering spectacular views of the island and the sea. You can also visit the botanical garden and the environmental centre of the park to learn more about its biodiversity.

The Cypress Trail: This is a circular trail that starts and ends in the picturesque village of Fiskardo, on the northern tip of Kefalonia. The trail passes through a forest of cypress trees, olive groves, and vineyards, as well as some traditional villages and churches. You can also enjoy panoramic views of the Ionian Sea and the neighbouring islands of Ithaca and Lefkada. The trail is about 5 km long and takes about 2 hours to complete.

The Assos Castle Trail: This is a short but steep trail that leads to the Venetian castle of Assos, on the west coast of Kefalonia. The castle was built in the 16th century and was used as a fortress and a prison until the 19th century. The trail starts from the village of Assos, which is a charming fishing port with colourful houses and a pebbly beach. The trail climbs up to the castle, passing by some ruins and a chapel. From the castle, you can admire the views of Assos Bay and the peninsula, as well as the Myrtos beach in the distance. The trail is about 2 km long and takes about an hour to complete.

Boating in Kefalonia

Below are some of the boating options that you can enjoy in Kefalonia:

Renting a boat: If you want to have more freedom and flexibility, you can rent a boat and navigate the waters yourself. You can find several boat rental services in various locations on the island, such as Agia Efimia, Fiskardo, Lassi, and Skala. You can rent a boat for a few hours or a whole day, and you don't need a license or experience to drive it. You will be given a map and instructions on how to operate the boat and where to go. You can visit secluded beaches and wonderful coves, accessible only by boat. You can also bring your food and drinks, or stop at a taverna along the way. Some of the boat rental services are Yellow Boats Kefalonia, Boulevard Boat Hire Kefalonia, and Lassi Rent A Boat.

Joining a cruise: If you prefer to join a group and have a guide, you can join a cruise that will take you to some of the most beautiful places around Kefalonia. You can find various cruises that depart from different ports on the island, such as Argostoli, Sami, Fiskardo, and Poros. You can visit places such as Ithaca, Lefkada, Zakynthos, Melissani Cave, Myrtos Beach, and Assos.

You can also enjoy swimming, snorkelling, sunbathing, and sightseeing. Some of the cruises include food and drinks on board, as well as live music and entertainment. Some of the cruise companies are Kefalonia Trips, Dreamy Cruises, and Ionian Discoveries.

Taking a ferry: If you want to visit another island for a longer time, you can take a ferry that will transport you and your vehicle. You can find ferry services that connect Kefalonia with other islands such as Ithaca, Zakynthos, Lefkada, Corfu, and Kythira. You can also take a ferry to the mainland of Greece or Italy. You can book your tickets online or at the port. Some of the ferry companies are Ionian Group, Levante Ferries, and Kefalonian Lines.

Snorkelling in Kefalonia

Snorkelling in Kefalonia is a fun and exciting activity that will allow you to discover the underwater beauty of the Ionian Sea. Kefalonia has many spots where you can snorkel, from secluded coves and rocky beaches to sea caves and sunken villages. You can see a variety of marine life, such as fish, crabs, octopus, sea urchins, starfish, and even turtles. You can also admire the colourful corals, sponges, and seaweeds that decorate the seabed. Below are some of the best snorkelling spots in Kefalonia that you should not miss:

Asos Beach: This is a small and charming beach in the village of Asos, on the north of Argostoli. The beach has clear and calm waters that are ideal for snorkelling. You can explore the rocky left side of the beach, where you can find a cave and a variety of fish. You can also enjoy the scenic views of the Venetian castle that overlooks the bay.

Myrtos Beach: This is one of the most famous and beautiful beaches in Kefalonia, with white pebbles and turquoise waters. The beach is surrounded by white cliffs and green vegetation, creating a stunning contrast. The water is usually clear and deep, making it a good spot for snorkelling. You can see fish, crabs, and sea urchins along the rocky edges of the beach.

Petani Beach: This is another stunning beach on the west coast of Kefalonia, near the village of Vovikes. The beach has golden sand and blue-green waters that sparkle in the sun. The water is deep and clear, offering excellent visibility for snorkelling. You can explore the rocky right side of the beach, where you can find a small cave and a lot of fish.

Kimilia Beach: This is a hidden gem on the north-east coast of Kefalonia, near the village of Emblisi. The beach is accessible only by boat or by a hiking trail through the forest. The beach has white sand and crystal-clear waters that are perfect for snorkelling. You can see corals, sponges, starfish, and fish in the shallow waters.

Dafnoudi Beach: This is a secluded beach on the northeast coast of Kefalonia, near the village of Fiskardo. The beach is reachable by boat or by a walking path through an olive grove. The beach has pebbles and clear waters that are ideal for snorkelling. You can see fish, octopus, sea urchins, and seaweeds in the water.

Turtle Spotting in Kefalonia

Turtle spotting in Kefalonia is a wonderful activity that will allow you to see these amazing creatures in their natural habitat. Kefalonia is home to the loggerhead turtle (Caretta caretta), which is an endangered species that nests and forages on the island's beaches and bays. Below are some tips and information for turtle spotting in Kefalonia:

The best time to see turtles in Kefalonia is between May and August when they arrive on the island to mate and lay their eggs. You may also see them in September and October when the hatchlings emerge from their nests and make their way to the sea.

The best place to see turtles in Kefalonia is Argostoli Bay, where they feed every morning in the shallow waters. You can see them from the bridge or the promenade, or you can take a boat tour or rent a kayak to get closer to them. You may also spot them near the fishing boats, where they wait for scraps of fish.

Other places where you can see turtles in Kefalonia are Turtle Beach in Lassi, Monastery Beach, Myrtos Beach, Agia Efimia Beach, and Koroni Beach. These are some of the nesting beaches where the female turtles come ashore at night to dig their nests and lay their eggs. You may also see the hatchlings crawling out of the sand and heading to the water.

If you want to learn more about the turtles and their conservation, you can visit the Katelios Group, a local organization that monitors and protects the turtle population in Kefalonia. You can join their guided tours, volunteer programs, or educational activities.

If you do see turtles, be sure to respect them and their environment. Do not touch, feed, or disturb them in any way. Do not use flash photography or bright lights. Do not leave any litter or damage any vegetation. Follow the instructions of the local authorities and the Katelios Group.

Turtle spotting in Kefalonia is a unique and memorable experience that will make you appreciate these beautiful animals and their importance to the ecosystem. You will not only have fun and learn new things but also contribute to their protection and survival. Happy turtle spotting!

Wine Tasting in Kefalonia

There are several ways to enjoy wine tasting in Kefalonia, depending on your preferences and budget. You can:

Rent a car or a bike and explore the island's vineyards and wineries on your own. You can visit some of the most famous wineries, such as Gentilini Winery, Sarris Winery, Divino Wines and Vinegar, Orealios, Sclavos Wines, Petrakopoulos Wines, Haritatos Vineyard, and Domaine Foivos. You can taste their wines, learn about their history and production process, and buy some bottles to take home. You can also enjoy the views of the mountains, the sea, and the countryside along the way.

Join a guided tour or a cruise that will take you to some of the best wine-tasting spots on the island. You can find various tours and cruises that depart from different ports on the island, such as Argostoli, Sami, Fiskardo, and Poros. You can visit places such as Ithaca, Lefkada, Zakynthos, Melissani Cave, Myrtos Beach, and Assos. You can also enjoy swimming, snorkelling, sunbathing, and sightseeing. Some of the tours and cruises include food and drinks on board, as well as live music and entertainment. Some of the tour and cruise companies are Kefalonia Trips, Dreamy Cruises, Ionian Discoveries, and The Greek Wine Experience.

Take a wine-tasting class or a workshop that will teach you more about the wines of Kefalonia and Greece. You can learn how to taste wine properly, how to pair wine with food, how to make your wine or vinegar, and how to improve your wine knowledge. You can also taste different wines from different regions and varieties, as well as local cheeses and snacks. Some of the places that offer wine-tasting classes or workshops are Viva Your

Personal Chef, Taste Kefalonia Food Experience at Sea Rock ws, Katia Stefanatou, and Kefalonia Wine Tour.

Chapter 7 • Shopping in Kefalonia

Fashion and Luxury Shopping

Fashion and luxury shopping in Kefalonia is not very common, as the island is more known for its natural beauty and traditional products. However, there are some places where you can find high-quality clothes, accessories, and jewellery, as well as local handicrafts and souvenirs. Below are some of the best places for fashion and luxury shopping in Kefalonia:

Christine Mar: This is a boutique that offers a selection of elegant and stylish clothes, shoes, bags, and accessories from Greek and international designers. The boutique is located on the main street of Argostoli, near the central square. You can find brands such as Max Mara, Liu Jo, Twinset, Guess, and more. The staff is friendly and helpful, and the prices are reasonable for the quality.

Tzannatos Jewellers: This is a family-run business that has been operating since 1916. The shop is located on Lithostroto Street in Argostoli. You can find a variety of jewellery, watches, and accessories made of gold, silver, diamonds, pearls, and other precious stones. You can also find handmade jewellery inspired by the Kefalonian culture and history. The shop also offers repair and engraving services.

DeKacreations: This is a shop that sells handmade leather goods, such as bags, wallets, belts, and sandals. The shop is located in the village of Lixouri. You can choose from different colours, styles, and sizes, or order a custom-made product. The leather is of high quality and the craftsmanship is excellent. The shop also sells other items such as hats, scarves, and sunglasses.

Selene Arts & Crafts: This is a shop that sells handmade ceramics, paintings, sculptures, and other artworks by local artists. The shop is located in the village of Fiskardo. You can find unique and original pieces that reflect the island's beauty and culture. You can also watch the artists at work in their studio or join a pottery workshop.

Kefalonian Product Boutique: This is a shop that sells organic and natural products from Kefalonia and other parts of Greece. The shop is located in the village of Karavados. You can find products such as honey, olive oil, wine, vinegar, cheese, herbs, spices, cosmetics, and more. You can also see tools and equipment used in farming dating from 1930. The shop also offers tasting sessions and cooking classes.

Local Markets and Souvenirs

If you are looking for local markets and souvenirs in Kefalonia, you have plenty of options to choose from. You can find a variety of products that reflect the island's culture, history, and nature, such as honey, wine, cheese, olive oil, herbs, spices, ceramics, jewellery, leather goods, and more. Below are some of the best places to shop for local markets and souvenirs in Kefalonia:

Argostoli Central Market: This is a lively and colourful market that takes place every morning on the waterfront of Argostoli, the capital of Kefalonia. You can find fresh fruits, vegetables, fish, meat, cheese, eggs, and other local produce. You can also find stalls selling honey, olive oil, wine, vinegar, spices, and sweets. The market is a great place to mingle with the locals and taste the authentic flavours of Kefalonia.

Fiskardo Artisan Market: This is a charming and quaint market that takes place every Sunday from June to September in the village of Fiskardo, on the north of Kefalonia. You can find handmade crafts and artworks by local artists, such as paintings, sculptures, ceramics, jewellery, leather goods, and more. You can also enjoy live music and entertainment by local performers.

Skala Street Market: This is a fun market that takes place every Thursday evening from May to October in the village of Skala, in the south of Kefalonia. You can find clothes, accessories, souvenirs, and gifts from various vendors. You can also find local delicacies such as honey, cheese, olives, nuts, and pastries. The market is a great place to enjoy the nightlife and atmosphere of Skala.

Myrtillo: This is a fabulous little shop that sells honey and other bee products from Kefalonia. The shop is located in the village of Poulata, near the Melissani Cave. You can find different types of honey, such as black pine honey, thyme honey, heather honey, and orange blossom honey. You can also find beeswax candles, soaps, cosmetics, and more. The shop also has a cafe where you can enjoy coffee and snacks made with honey.

These are some of the best local markets in Kefalonia. You can find quality products that suit your taste and style, as well as support the local economy and culture. Happy shopping!

Artisan Crafts and Workshops

Below are some of the best workshops that you can visit in Kefalonia:

Weaving Workshop: This is a hands-on workshop that will teach you how to weave using traditional loom and natural materials. You will learn about the history and techniques of weaving from different regions of Greece, as well as how to make your patterns and designs. You will also get to take home your woven product, such as a scarf, a bag, or a rug.

Ceramics Workshop: This is a fun and creative workshop that will teach you how to make your pottery using clay and a pottery wheel. You will learn about the basics of pottery making, such as shaping, glazing, and firing. You will also get to see some examples of local ceramic art, such as plates, cups, and vases.

Leather Workshop: This is a practical and enjoyable workshop that will teach you how to make your leather goods, such as bags, wallets, belts, and sandals. You will learn about the different types of leather, how to cut, sew, and dye them, and how to add your personal touch. You will also get to see some examples of local leather crafts, such as hats, jackets, and shoes.

Jewelry Workshop: This is a fascinating and elegant workshop that will teach you how to make your jewellery using silver, gold, pearls, and other precious stones. You will learn about the different styles and techniques of jewellery making, such as wire wrapping, beading, and soldering. You will also get to see some examples of local jewellery art, such as rings, earrings, necklaces, and bracelets.

Honey Workshop: This is an informative workshop that will teach you about the production and benefits of honey and other bee products. You will learn about the life cycle and behaviour of bees, how they make honey and wax, and how they pollinate plants. You will also get to taste different types of honey from Kefalonia and other parts of Greece.

Antique and Vintage Shopping

Antique and vintage shopping in Kefalonia is not very common, as the island is more known for its natural beauty and traditional products. However, there are some places where you can find some interesting and unique items from the past, such as furniture, books, clothes, jewellery, and more. Below are some of the best places for antique and vintage shopping in Kefalonia:

The Old Bookstore: This is a cosy and charming bookstore that sells old and rare books, maps, prints, and posters. The bookstore is located on Lithostroto Street in Argostoli. You can find books from different genres, languages, and periods, as well as some collector's items and first editions. The owner is very knowledgeable and friendly and can help you find what you are looking for.

The Antique Shop: This is a small and eclectic shop that sells antique furniture, lamps, mirrors, clocks, paintings, and other decorative items. The shop is located on the main road between Argostoli and Lassi. You can find items from different styles and eras, such as Art Deco, Art Nouveau, Victorian, and more. The shop also offers restoration and repair services.

The Vintage Shop: This is a trendy and stylish shop that sells vintage clothes, accessories, shoes, and bags. The shop is located on the main street of Skala. You can find clothes from different decades, such as the 50s, 60s, 70s, and 80s, as well as some designer labels and brands. The shop also sells handmade jewellery and gifts made from recycled materials.

The Flea Market: This is a lively and fun market that takes place every Saturday morning in the village of Lixouri. You can find a variety of items from local sellers, such as clothes, shoes, books, records, CDs, DVDs, toys, games, tools, and more. You can also bargain with the sellers and get some good deals. The market is a great place to mingle with the locals and enjoy the atmosphere.

Chapter 8 • Practical Information

Health and Safety Tips

Below are some tips to help you enjoy your trip to Kefalonia safely and comfortably:

Travel insurance: You should take out comprehensive travel and medical insurance to cover you while you're away. This will protect you in case of any accidents, illnesses, or emergencies that may occur during your trip. You should also check what your insurance covers and excludes, and keep a copy of your policy and contact details with you at all times.

Health care: If you're travelling to the EU and you apply for a card now, you'll get a new UK Global Health Insurance Card (GHIC) instead of an EHIC. This entitles you to emergency medical treatment on the same terms as Greek nationals. It won't, however, cover you for medical repatriation, ongoing medical treatment or non-urgent treatment. You do not need to apply for a GHIC if you already have an EHIC. Your EHIC remains valid in the EU until it expires. An EHIC or GHIC is free of charge.

Sun protection: Kefalonia has a hot and sunny climate, especially in the summer months. You should protect yourself from the sun by wearing sunscreen, sunglasses, a hat, and light clothing. You should also drink plenty of water to avoid dehydration and heatstroke. Avoid staying in the sun for too long, especially between 11 a.m. and 3 p.m., when the sun is strong.

Water safety: Kefalonia has many beautiful beaches and bays where you can swim, snorkel, or boat. However, you should be careful of the water conditions and currents, which can change quickly. You should also follow the flag system on the beaches, which indicates the level of safety: green means safe, yellow means caution, red means danger, and black means no swimming. You should also wear a life jacket when boating or kayaking, and avoid swimming alone or at night.

Food safety: Kefalonia has a delicious and varied cuisine that uses fresh and local ingredients. However, you should be careful of what you eat and drink, especially if you have any allergies or dietary restrictions. You should avoid eating raw or undercooked meat, fish, eggs, or dairy products. You should also avoid drinking tap water or ice cubes, as they may not be safe or taste good. You should drink bottled water instead, which is cheap and widely available.

Road safety: Kefalonia has a good road network that connects the main towns and villages on the island. However, some roads are narrow, winding, steep, or poorly maintained. You should drive carefully and defensively, and follow the traffic rules and signs. You should also wear a seat belt at all times, and avoid driving under the influence of alcohol or drugs. If you rent a car or a bike, you should check that it is in good condition and has insurance.

Crime prevention: Kefalonia is generally a safe and peaceful island with low crime rates. However, you should still take some precautions to prevent theft or loss of your valuables. You should keep your passport, money, cards, and tickets in a safe place or on your person. You should also lock your hotel room or apartment when you leave it. You should avoid carrying large amounts of cash or wearing expensive jewellery. You should also be aware of your surroundings and avoid any suspicious or unsafe situations.

Emergency Contacts

Emergency contacts are important to have in case of any accidents, illnesses, or emergencies that may occur during your trip to Kefalonia. Below are some of the emergency contacts that you should know and save:

Emergency Telephone code Greece: +30

Police Emergency: 100

First Aid: 166

Fire Department: 199

Forestry Aid: 191

Coast Guard: 108

Touristic Police: 171

Argostoli General Hospital: +30 2671 361100

Health Centre of Sami: +30 26740 22222

Hospital of Lixouri: +26713 60308

Argostoli Police Station: +30 26710 27821

Tourist Police in Argostoli: +30 26710 22815

Lixouri Police Station: +30 26710 91207

Sami Police Station: +30 26740 22100

Fiscardo Police Station: +30 26740 41460

Ithaca Police Station: +30 26740 32205

Argostoli Port Authority: +30 26710 22224

Lixouri Port Authority: +30 26710 94100

Sami Port Authority: +30 26740 22031

Poros Port Authority: +30 26740 72460

Ithaca Port Authority: +30 26743 60640

Fiscardo Port Authority: +30 26740 41400

You should also take out comprehensive travel and medical insurance to cover you while you're away, and check what your insurance covers and excludes. You should also apply for a UK Global Health Insurance Card (GHIC) or use your existing European Health Insurance Card (EHIC) if you're travelling to the EU, as this entitles you to emergency medical treatment on the same terms as Greek nationals.

We hope that you will have a safe and enjoyable trip to Kefalonia, but in case of any emergencies, you can use these contacts to get help and assistance. Remember to have fun and respect the nature and culture of Kefalonia. Happy travels!

Communication and Internet Access

Below are some of the options that you can use for communication and internet access in Kefalonia:

Mobile phone: You can use your mobile phone in Kefalonia, as the island has good coverage of GSM and 3G networks. However, you should check with your provider about the roaming charges and plans that apply to your phone. You may also need to activate international roaming before you travel. Alternatively, you can buy a local SIM card from one of the Greek mobile operators, such as Cosmote, Vodafone, or Wind. You can find their shops or kiosks in the main towns and villages on the island. You can also buy prepaid cards or top up your credit online or at various outlets.

Landline phone: You can use landline phones in Kefalonia, as the island has a reliable and affordable telephone service. You can find public phones in the streets, squares, or shops on the island. You can use coins or cards to make local or international calls. You can also use landline phones in your hotel or apartment, but you may need to pay extra charges for the calls. The country code for Greece is +30, and the area code for Kefalonia is 2671.

Internet access: You can access the internet in Kefalonia, as the island has a wide range of internet services and providers. You can find free WiFi access in most hotels, cafes, bars, restaurants, and tavernas on the island. However, you should be careful of the security and speed of these connections. You can also find internet cafes or kiosks in the main towns and villages on the island, where you can use computers or laptops for a fee. Alternatively, you can use mobile data or rent a portable WiFi device from one of the local providers. Another option is to use Kefalonia Broadband, which is a wireless internet service that covers most areas on the island. You can pay as you go or subscribe to a monthly plan.

Chapter 9 • Recommended Itineraries

One day in Kefalonia

One day in Kefalonia is not enough to see and do everything that this beautiful island has to offer, but you can still make the most of it by following this itinerary. This itinerary will take you to some of the most popular and scenic attractions in Kefalonia, as well as give you a taste of the island's culture and cuisine. Below is a suggested one-day in Kefalonia itinerary:

Start your day with a visit to the Melissani Cave, a stunning underground lake that is illuminated by the sun. You can take a boat tour inside the cave and admire the crystal-clear water and the colourful stalactites and stalagmites. The cave is located near the town of Sami, and you can get there by car or by bus.

After exploring the Melissani Cave, head to the nearby Antisamos Beach, one of the most beautiful beaches in Kefalonia. The beach has white pebbles and turquoise waters that are perfect for swimming and snorkelling. You can also relax on the sunbeds or enjoy a drink at the beach bar. The beach is also famous for being one of the filming locations of the movie Captain Corelli's Mandolin.

For lunch, you can either stay at Antisamos Beach or drive to the town of Agia Efimia, a charming fishing port with many tavernas and cafes. You can try some of the local specialities, such as kreatopita (meat pie), riganada (bread with cheese and oregano), or bakaliaros skordalia (fried cod with garlic sauce). You can also taste some of the local wines, such as Robola or Mavrodaphne.

In the afternoon, drive to the town of Fiskardo, on the north of Kefalonia. Fiskardo is one of the few towns that survived the 1953 earthquake, and it has colourful architecture. You can stroll along the waterfront and see the fishing boats and yachts, or visit some of the shops and boutiques that sell local crafts and souvenirs. You can also take a boat trip to the nearby islands of Ithaca or Lefkada.

For dinner, you can either stay in Fiskardo or drive back to Argostoli, the capital of Kefalonia. Argostoli has a lively and cosmopolitan atmosphere, with many restaurants, bars, and clubs. You can find a variety of cuisines, from Greek to Italian to Chinese. You can also enjoy some nightlife and entertainment in Argostoli, such as live music, theatre, or cinema.

This is a sample one-day Kefalonia itinerary that will give you an overview of what this island has to offer. Of course, you can modify it according to your preferences and interests. You can also extend your stay in Kefalonia and explore more of its attractions, such as Myrtos Beach, Assos Village, Mount Ainos National Park, and more. Whatever you choose to do, you will surely have a memorable time in Kefalonia.

Three days in Kefalonia

Three days in Kefalonia is a good amount of time to see some of the highlights of this beautiful Greek island. You can enjoy its stunning beaches, charming villages, natural wonders, and delicious cuisine. Below is a suggested three days in Kefalonia itinerary that you can follow or modify according to your preferences and interests:

Day 1: Explore the north of Kefalonia

Start your day with a visit to the Melissani Cave. After exploring the Melissani Cave, head to the nearby

Antisamos Beach. For lunch, you can either stay at Antisamos Beach or drive to the town of Agia Efimia. You can try some of the local specialities. In the afternoon, drive to the town of Fiskardo, on the north of Kefalonia. For dinner, you can either stay in Fiskardo or drive back to Argostoli, the capital of Kefalonia.

Day 2: Discover the west of Kefalonia

Start your day with a visit to Myrtos Beach, one of the most famous and beautiful beaches in Kefalonia. After enjoying Myrtos Beach, drive to Assos Village, one of the most picturesque and romantic villages in Kefalonia. For lunch, you can either stay in Assos Village or drive to Petani Beach, another stunning beach on the west coast of Kefalonia. In the afternoon, drive to Lixouri, the second-largest town in Kefalonia. For dinner, you can either stay in Lixouri or drive back to Argostoli. You can find more options for dining and entertainment in both towns.

Day 3: Enjoy Kefalonia's stunning landscape

Start your day with a visit to Ainos National Park, which is home to the highest peak of Kefalonia, Mount Ainos (or Mount Aenos). After exploring Ainos National Park, drive to the village of Peratata. For lunch, you can either stay in Peratata or drive to Gentilini Winery, one of the most famous and oldest wineries in Kefalonia. In the afternoon, drive to Skala, one of the most popular and lively resorts in Kefalonia. For dinner, you can either stay in Skala or drive back to Argostoli. You can find more options for dining and entertainment in both places.

This is a sample three-day Kefalonia itinerary that will give you an overview of what this island has to offer. Of course, you can modify it according to your preferences and interests. You can also extend your stay in Kefalonia and explore more of its attractions, such as Dafnoudi Beach, Fteri Beach, Koroni Beach, and more. Whatever you choose to do, you will surely have a memorable time in Kefalonia.

Five days in Kefalonia

Five days in Kefalonia is a perfect amount of time to enjoy the beauty and diversity of this Greek island. You can visit its stunning beaches, charming villages, natural wonders, and historical monuments, as well as taste its delicious cuisine and wine. Below is a suggested five days in Kefalonia itinerary that you can follow or modify according to your preferences and interests:

Day 1: Explore the north of Kefalonia

Start your day with a visit to the Melissani Cave. After exploring the Melissani Cave, head to the nearby Antisamos Beach. For lunch, you can either stay at Antisamos Beach or drive to the town of Agia Efimia, a charming fishing port with many tavernas and cafes. In the afternoon, drive to the town of Fiskardo, on the north of Kefalonia. For dinner, you can either stay in Fiskardo or drive back to Argostoli, the capital of Kefalonia.

Day 2: Discover the west of Kefalonia

Start your day with a visit to Myrtos Beach. After enjoying Myrtos Beach, drive to Assos Village. For lunch, you can either stay in Assos Village or drive to Petani Beach, another stunning beach on the west coast of Kefalonia. In the afternoon, drive to Lixouri, the second-largest town in Kefalonia. For dinner, you can either stay in Lixouri or drive back to Argostoli. You can find more options for dining and entertainment in both towns.

Day 3: Enjoy Kefalonia's stunning landscape

Start your day with a visit to Ainos National Park, which is home to the highest peak of Kefalonia, Mount Ainos (or Mount Aenos). After exploring Ainos National Park, drive to the village of Peratata. For lunch, you can either stay in Peratata or drive to Gentilini Winery. In the afternoon, drive to Skala, one of the most popular and lively resorts in Kefalonia. For dinner, you can either stay in Skala or drive back to Argostoli.

Day 4: Visit Ithaca, Kefalonia's sister island

Start your day with a ferry ride from Sami or Fiskardo to Ithaca, Kefalonia's sister island. Ithaca is a small and peaceful island that is famous for being the home of Odysseus, the hero of Homer's epic poem The Odyssey.

After arriving in Ithaca, visit the Cave of Nymphs, where Odysseus hid his treasures when he returned from his long journey. The cave is located near the village of Polis, and you can see some stalactites, stalagmites, and a small lake inside. You can also see some inscriptions on the walls that date back to ancient times.

Next, visit the Archaeological Museum of Ithaca, where you can see some artefacts and exhibits that showcase the island's history and culture. The museum is located in the town of Vathy, which is also the capital and main port of Ithaca. You can see items such as pottery, coins, statues, jewellery, and weapons from different periods.

For lunch, you can either stay in Vathy or drive to Kioni, a picturesque village on the east coast of Ithaca. You can find some tavernas and cafes that serve fresh seafood and local dishes. You can also enjoy the views of the bay and the colourful houses.

In the afternoon, drive to Stavros, a village on the north of Ithaca. Here you can visit the bust of Odysseus, which is a symbol of the island's identity and pride. You can also visit the Church of Agios Nikolaos (St. Nicholas), which has a beautiful bell tower and a wooden iconostasis.

For dinner, you can either stay in Stavros or drive back to Vathy.

Day 5: Relax on Kefalonia's best beaches

On your last day in Kefalonia, you can relax on some of the island's best beaches that you may have missed or want to revisit. You can choose from different types of beaches. You can continue your itinerary by visiting some of the following beaches:

Emblisi Beach

Fteri Beach

Koroni Beach

These are some of the best beaches that you can relax on your last day in Kefalonia. You can also revisit some of the beaches that you have already visited or explore some other beaches that you may have missed.

Whatever you choose to do, you will surely enjoy the beauty and tranquillity of Kefalonia's coastline. Happy travels!

Chapter 10 • Travelling with Children

Family-Friendly Attractions

Below are some of the best family-friendly attractions in Kefalonia:

Myrtos Beach: This is one of the most famous and scenic beaches in Greece, with turquoise waters and white pebbles. It is ideal for swimming, sunbathing, and taking photos. However, it is not very suitable for young children, as the water gets deep quickly and the waves can be strong. If you decide to visit this beach, make sure to supervise your kids at all times.

Melissani Cave: This is a natural wonder that will amaze you and your kids. It is a cave with an underground lake that has crystal clear water and a hole in the roof that lets the sunlight in. You can take a boat tour inside the cave and admire the stunning colours and formations. The cave is also connected to Greek mythology, as it was believed to be the home of nymphs.

Petani Beach: This is another beautiful beach that has golden sand and clear blue water. It is more family-friendly than Myrtos Beach, as it has shallow water and gentle waves. It also has sunbeds, umbrellas, and tavernas nearby. You can relax on the beach, play with your kids, or enjoy some water sports.

Assos: This is a picturesque village that is located on a small peninsula surrounded by the sea. It has a Venetian castle on the top of the hill that offers panoramic views of the area. You can walk around the village, explore the castle, or swim in the calm bay. The village has a cosy atmosphere and a few shops and cafes.

Antisamos Beach: This is a popular beach that was featured in the movie Captain Corelli's Mandolin. It has green hills behind it and clear water in front of it. It is a great place for snorkelling, as you can see many fish and marine life. It also has sunbeds, umbrellas, and a beach bar.

Kaminia Beach: This is a long and sandy beach that is ideal for families with young children. It has shallow water and no waves, making it safe and easy for kids to swim. It is also a nesting site for loggerhead turtles, so you might be lucky enough to see some of them. The beach has a few tavernas and a turtle rescue centre.

Dias Beekeeping: This is a fun and educational attraction that will teach you and your kids about bees and honey production. You can visit the bee farm, see the hives, taste different types of honey, and learn about the benefits of honey for health and beauty. You can also buy some honey products as souvenirs.

Skala Beach: This is a lively and well-organized beach that has everything you need for a perfect day. It has fine sand, clear water, sunbeds, umbrellas, showers, changing rooms, and water sports facilities. You can also find many restaurants, bars, shops, and hotels nearby. The beach is suitable for all ages and preferences.

Emplisi Beach: This is a secluded and peaceful beach that is located near Fiskardo village. It has white pebbles and turquoise water that contrast with the green cliffs around it. It is a good spot for snorkelling, as you can see many colourful fish. The beach has no facilities, so you need to bring your supplies.

Makris Gialos Beach: This is a sandy beach that is close to Argostoli town. It has clear water and moderate waves that make it fun for swimming and playing. It also has sunbeds, umbrellas, showers, changing rooms, and a snack bar. The beach is popular among locals and tourists alike.

Child-Friendly Accommodation

Below are some recommendations:

White Rocks Hotel Kefalonia: This is a luxury resort that is located on the edge of a cliff, overlooking the stunning Platis Gialos beach. It has a private beach, a protected pine forest, and Venetian-style architecture that blends with the natural beauty of the surroundings. The resort offers spacious and elegant rooms and suites, some of which have floor-to-ceiling windows and glass balustrades that provide uninterrupted views of the sea. The resort also has a variety of facilities and services for families, such as a kid's pool, a playground, a game room, and babysitting. You can also enjoy the delicious cuisine at the restaurant, the refreshing drinks at the beach bar, or the relaxing treatments at the spa.

Lassi Hotel: This is a family-run hotel that is situated just 60 meters from the harbour and beaches of Agia Efimia. It has 89 comfortable rooms that have a refrigerator, a TV, and air conditioning. The hotel also offers free Wi-Fi, free parking, and free buffet breakfast. You can also enjoy the outdoor pool, the garden, or the terrace. The hotel is close to many attractions, such as Melissani Cave, Myrtos Beach, and Antisamos Beach.

Limanaki Hotel: This is another family-friendly hotel that is located in Lassi, near Agioi Theodoroi Beach. It has 32 cosy rooms that have a refrigerator, a minibar, and air conditioning. The hotel also offers free Wi-Fi, free parking, and free breakfast. You can also relax at the outdoor pool, the lounge, or the snack bar. The hotel is near many restaurants, bars, shops, and hotels.

Mounda Beach Hotel: This is a charming hotel that is located near Skala Beach, which is a nesting site for loggerhead turtles. It has 18 bright rooms that have a balcony or terrace with sea or mountain views. The hotel also offers free Wi-Fi, free parking, and free breakfast. You can also enjoy the garden or the library. The hotel is eco-friendly and supports turtle conservation projects.

Studios Diamanto: This is a modern hotel that is located in Karavomylos village, near Sami town. It has 12 studios that have a kitchenette, a TV, and air conditioning. The hotel also offers free Wi-Fi, free parking, and an outdoor pool. You can also enjoy the barbecue facilities or the bicycle rentals. The hotel is close to Melissani Cave and Antisamos Beach.

These are some of the best child-friendly accommodations in Kefalonia.

Chapter 11 • Travelling on a Budget

Budget-Friendly Accommodation

Kefalonia is a wonderful destination for travellers who want to enjoy the beauty and culture of Greece without spending too much money. Many budget-friendly accommodations on the island offer comfort, convenience, and quality services. Below are some of the best budget-friendly hotels in Kefalonia:

Lassi Hotel: This is a family-run hotel that is situated just 60 meters from the harbour and beaches of Agia Efimia. It has 89 comfortable rooms that have a refrigerator, a TV, and air conditioning. The hotel also offers free Wi-Fi, free parking, and free buffet breakfast. You can also enjoy the outdoor pool, the garden, or the terrace. The hotel is close to many attractions, such as Melissani Cave, Myrtos Beach, and Antisamos Beach.

Hotel Oceanis: This is another family-friendly hotel that is located in Lassi, near Agioi Theodoroi Beach. It has 32 cosy rooms that have a refrigerator, a minibar, and air conditioning. The hotel also offers free Wi-Fi, free parking, and free breakfast. You can also relax at the outdoor pool, the lounge, or the snack bar. The hotel is near many restaurants, bars, shops, and hotels.

Hotel Summary: This is a 3-star hotel that is located in Lixouri, offering affordable and good quality holidays since 1981. It has 69 spacious and elegant rooms and suites, some of which have floor-to-ceiling windows and glass balustrades that provide uninterrupted views of the sea. The hotel also has a variety of facilities and services for families, such as a kid's pool, a playground, a game room, and babysitting. You can also enjoy the delicious cuisine at the restaurant, the refreshing drinks at the beach bar, or the relaxing treatments at the spa.

Mounda Beach Hotel: This is a charming hotel that is located near Skala Beach, which is a nesting site for loggerhead turtles. It has 18 bright rooms that have a balcony or terrace with sea or mountain views. The hotel also offers free Wi-Fi, free parking, and free breakfast. You can also enjoy the garden or the library. The hotel is eco-friendly and supports turtle conservation projects.

Studios Diamanto: This is a modern hotel that is located in Karavomylos village, near Sami town. It has

12 studios that have a kitchenette, a TV, and air conditioning. The hotel also offers free Wi-Fi, free parking, and an outdoor pool. You can also enjoy the barbecue facilities or the bicycle rentals. The hotel is close to Melissani Cave and Antisamos Beach.

Cheap Eats and Local Food

If you are looking for cheap eats and local food in Kefalonia, below are some of the best places to try:

Ladokolla: This is a fast food restaurant that specializes in grilled meat wrapped in greaseproof paper (ladokolla). You can choose from different types of meat, such as pork, chicken, lamb, or beef, and add various sauces and salads. The portions are generous and the prices are low. You can find Ladokolla in Argostoli and Lixouri.

Taverna Patsouras: This is a family-run taverna that serves authentic Greek food in a cosy and friendly atmosphere. You can enjoy dishes such as moussaka, stuffed tomatoes, lamb kleftiko, fried cheese, and grilled octopus. The taverna also offers a daily special menu that changes according to the season and the availability of ingredients. The taverna is located in Agia Efimia.

Steki Grill: This is a popular grill house that offers delicious seafood and meat dishes at reasonable prices. You can try the fresh fish of the day, the squid rings, the shrimp saganaki, or the souvlaki. The grill house also has a salad bar and a variety of appetizers. The grill house is located in Poros.

Tsobos Garden Grillhouse: This is another grill house that serves amazing meaty treats in a beautiful garden setting. You can order the mixed grill platter, which includes pork chops, chicken fillets, sausages, burgers, and kebabs. You can also try the lamb ribs, the beef steak, or the pork tenderloin. The grill house is located in Lourdata.

Sugar pastry shop: This is a sweet spot that offers a wide range of desserts and ice creams. You can indulge in cakes, pies, cookies, waffles, crepes, or doughnuts. You can also taste different flavours of ice cream, such as chocolate, vanilla, pistachio, or yoghurt. The pastry shop is located in Argostoli.

Free and Affordable Attractions

Below are some of them:

Myrtos Beach: The beach is free to access, but you may have to pay for parking or sunbeds.

Melissani Cave: The entrance fee for the cave is 7 euros for adults and 4 euros for children.

Assos: The village and the castle are free to visit, but you may have to pay for parking or refreshments.

Mount Ainos National Park: The park is free to enter, but you may need a 4x4 vehicle to access some parts of it.

Argostoli Harbour: The harbour and most of the attractions are free to visit, but you may have to pay for some museums or tours.

Transportation Tips for Saving Money

Below are some ways to save money on transportation in Kefalonia:

Rent a car: If you want to explore the island at your own pace and convenience, renting a car is the best option. However, car rental prices can vary depending on the season, the type of car, and the company. To save money, you should book your car in advance, compare different offers online, choose a smaller and more efficient car, and avoid any extra fees or charges.

Use public buses: If you don't mind travelling with the locals and following their schedule, public buses are a cheap and reliable way to get around the island. Most public bus trips will cost around $1.65 per ride and take you to the majority of larger towns and popular beaches.

Take a ferry: If you want to visit some of the neighbouring islands, such as Ithaca, Lefkada, Killini, or Zakynthos, taking a ferry is a fun and affordable way to do so. The ferry prices depend on the destination, the duration, and the type of vehicle or passenger. For example, a one-way trip from Kefalonia to Ithaca will cost $4 for a car and $2 for a passenger.

Walk or cycle: If you are staying in a small village or near a beach, walking or cycling can be a great way to enjoy the scenery and save money on transportation. You can also find some hiking or biking trails that will take you to some of the most beautiful spots on the island. You can rent a bike from some of the local shops or hotels, or bring your own if you have one.

Share a taxi: If you need to travel somewhere quickly or comfortably, taking a taxi can be an option. However, taxis can be expensive in Kefalonia, especially if you travel long distances or during peak hours. To save money, you can try to share a taxi with other travellers who are going to the same destination or direction. You can also negotiate the price with the driver before getting in.

Chapter 12 • Sustainability and Responsible Travel

Sustainable Tourism in Kefalonia

Sustainable tourism is a form of tourism that aims to minimize the negative impacts and maximize the positive benefits of tourism for the environment, society, and the economy. Sustainable tourism is especially important for islands, as they are more vulnerable to the pressures and challenges of tourism development. Kefalonia is a beautiful Greek island that offers many attractions for visitors but also faces some sustainability issues, such as poor accessibility, unfair competition, foreign investment dependence, and bureaucracy. Therefore, Kefalonia needs to adopt and promote sustainable tourism practices that will ensure the preservation and enhancement of its natural and cultural heritage, the well-being and empowerment of its local community, and the quality and competitiveness of its tourism products. Below are some ways to practice sustainable tourism in Kefalonia:

Choose eco-friendly accommodation: There are many hotels and resorts in Kefalonia that have adopted environmental measures, such as energy and water saving, waste management, recycling, organic farming, and green certification. By staying in these places, you can support their efforts and reduce your ecological footprint. Some examples of eco-friendly accommodation in Kefalonia are White Rocks Hotel Kefalonia, Hotel Summery, Mounda Beach Hotel, and Studios Diamanto.

Support local businesses: One of the best ways to contribute to the local economy and culture is to buy local products and services. You can shop at the local markets, where you can find fresh fruits, vegetables, cheese, honey, wine, and other delicacies. You can also eat at the local tavernas, where you can taste the traditional dishes of Kefalonia, such as the Kefalonian meat pie, the cod pie, the rabbit stifado, and the Iliad. You can also join some local tours or activities, such as hiking, cycling, beekeeping, or wine tasting. Some examples of local businesses in Kefalonia are Taverna

Patsouras, Dias Beekeeping, Kefalonia Tours, and Sugaro Pastry Shop.

Respect the environment: Kefalonia is blessed with a rich and diverse natural environment that includes stunning beaches, fascinating caves, protected forests, and unique wildlife. You can enjoy these natural wonders without harming them by following some simple rules. For example, you can avoid littering or leaving any traces behind; you can use biodegradable sunscreen and avoid touching or feeding any animals; you can follow the designated paths and avoid stepping on any plants; you can participate in some conservation projects or volunteer activities; and you can report any environmental problems or violations to the authorities.

Respect the culture: Kefalonia has a long and rich history that has shaped its culture and identity. You can learn more about the culture of Kefalonia by visiting some of its historical and cultural attractions, such as the Venetian castle in Assos, the Archaeological Museum in Argostoli, the Korgialenio Historical and Folklore Museum in Argostoli, and the Monastery of Agios Gerasimos. You can also respect the culture of Kefalonia by following some etiquette rules. For example, you can dress modestly when visiting religious sites; you can greet people with a smile and a "kalimera" (good morning) or a "kalispera" (good evening); you can accept any hospitality or gifts with gratitude; and you can avoid any sensitive topics or jokes.

Eco-Friendly Accommodation and Transportation

Below are some of the best eco-friendly accommodations and transportation in Kefalonia:

Eco-friendly accommodation: There are many hotels and resorts in Kefalonia that have adopted environmental measures, such as energy and water saving, waste management, recycling, organic farming, and green certification. By staying in these places, you can support their efforts and reduce your ecological footprint. Some examples of eco-friendly accommodation in Kefalonia are:

White Rocks Hotel Kefalonia: This is a luxury resort that is located on the edge of a cliff, overlooking the stunning Platis Gialos beach. It has a private beach, a protected pine forest, and Venetian-style architecture that blends with the natural beauty of the surroundings. The resort offers spacious and elegant rooms and suites, some of which have floor-to-ceiling windows and glass balustrades that provide uninterrupted views of the sea. The resort also has a variety of facilities and services for families, such as a kid's pool, a playground, a game room, and babysitting. You can also enjoy the delicious cuisine at the restaurant, the refreshing drinks at the beach bar, or the relaxing treatments at the spa.

Hotel Summary: This is a 3-star hotel that is located in Lixouri, offering affordable and good quality holidays since 1981. It has 69 spacious and elegant rooms and suites, some of which have floor-to-ceiling windows and glass balustrades that provide uninterrupted views of the sea. The hotel also has a variety of facilities and services for families, such as a kid's pool, a playground, a game room, and babysitting. The hotel also implements a water recycling policy, where used water is bio-mechanically cleaned and then re-used for watering purposes.

Mounda Beach Hotel: This is a charming hotel that is located near Skala Beach, which is a nesting site for loggerhead turtles. It has 18 bright rooms that have a balcony or terrace with sea or mountain views. The hotel also offers free Wi-Fi, free parking, and free breakfast.

You can also enjoy the garden or the library. The hotel is eco-friendly and supports turtle conservation projects.

Studios Diamanto: This is a modern hotel that is located in Karavomylos village, near Sami town. It has 12 studios that have a kitchenette, a TV, and air conditioning. The hotel also offers free Wi-Fi, free parking, and an outdoor pool. You can also enjoy the barbecue facilities or the bicycle rentals. The hotel uses solar energy to produce electricity and water heating.

Eco-friendly transportation: There are many ways to get around the island without harming the environment or spending too much money. Some examples of eco-friendly transportation in Kefalonia are:

Public buses: If you don't mind travelling with the locals and following their schedule, public buses are a cheap and reliable way to get around the island. Most public bus trips will cost around $1.65 per ride and take you to the majority of larger towns and popular beaches.

Ferry: If you want to visit some of the neighbouring islands, such as Ithaca, Lefkada, Killini, or Zakynthos, taking a ferry is a fun and affordable way to do so. The ferry prices depend on the destination, the duration, and the type of vehicle or passenger. For example, a one-way trip from Kefalonia to Ithaca will cost $4 for a car and $2 for a passenger.

Walking or cycling: If you are staying in a small village or near a beach, walking or cycling can be a great way to enjoy the scenery and save money on transportation. You can also find some hiking or biking trails that will take you to some of the most beautiful spots on the island. You can rent a bike from some of the local shops or hotels, or bring your own if you have one.

Ethical Experiences and Wildlife Conservation

Kefalonia is a beautiful island that is home to many wildlife species, such as sea turtles, monk seals, wild horses, and birds. If you are interested in ethical experiences and wildlife conservation, you can join some of the organizations and projects that are working to protect and study these animals and their habitats. Below are some of the best ethical experiences and wildlife conservation in Kefalonia:

Wildlife Sense: This is a research and conservation organization that is based on the island of Kefalonia. Their mission is to protect endangered sea turtles and their natural habitats, offer a unique learning experience to the volunteers who join their efforts and promote public awareness. They operate a science-based research and conservation project on the island, in collaboration with local and national authorities. You can join them as a volunteer and help them with tasks such as protecting sea turtle nests, monitoring sea turtle behaviour, studying seagrass meadows and dunes, and educating the public. You can also support them by donating or adopting a sea turtle.

Katelios Group: This is another research and conservation organization that is based on the island of Kefalonia. Their vision is to create a balance between tourism development and environmental protection. They focus on sea turtle conservation, environmental education, sustainable tourism, and cultural heritage. You can join them as a volunteer and help them with tasks such as patrolling the beaches, recording sea turtle data, cleaning the beaches, and organizing events. You can also support them by donating or becoming a member.

Kefalonia Tours: This is a tour company that offers eco-friendly and educational tours on the island of Kefalonia. They aim to show you the natural beauty and cultural diversity of the island while respecting the environment and the local community. You can choose from different tours, such as hiking, cycling, kayaking, snorkelling, or wine tasting. You can also join their special tours that focus on wildlife conservation, such as the turtle spotting tour or the monk seal tour.

Sugar pastry shop: This is a sweet spot that offers a wide range of desserts and ice creams. They also support wildlife conservation by donating part of their profits to Wildlife Sense and Katelios Group. You can indulge in cakes, pies, cookies, waffles, crepes, or doughnuts. You can also taste different flavours of ice cream, such as chocolate, vanilla, pistachio, or yoghurt.

Chapter 13 •
Accommodation in
Kefalonia

Hotel Recommendations

Below are some of the best luxury resort recommendations in Kefalonia:

F Zeen: This is an adults-only resort that is located near Lourdas Beach. It has 3 swimming pools, 2 fitness centres, and a spa. The rooms and suites are modern and elegant, with balconies or patios overlooking the sea or the garden. The resort also offers a restaurant, a beach bar, and a library. You can enjoy activities such as hiking, cycling, kayaking, or snorkelling.

Emelisse Nature Resort: This is a family-friendly resort that is located near Fiskardo village. It has an outdoor pool, a fitness centre, and a spa. The rooms and suites are spacious and cosy, with wooden furniture and natural colours. The resort also offers 2 restaurants, 2 bars, and an art gallery. You can enjoy activities such as tennis, yoga, or sailing.

White Rocks Hotel Kefalonia: This is a seafront resort that is located near Platis Gialos beach. It has a private beach, a protected pine forest, and a Venetian-style architecture. The rooms and suites are stylish and luxurious, with floor-to-ceiling windows and glass balustrades that provide uninterrupted views of the sea. The resort also offers a restaurant, a beach bar, and a spa.

Ionian Emerald Resort: This is a 5-star resort that is located near Karavomylos village. It has an outdoor pool, a fitness centre, and a spa. The rooms and suites are elegant and comfortable, with marble bathrooms and jacuzzi bathtubs. The resort also offers 2 restaurants, 2 bars, and a conference centre. You can enjoy activities such as water sports, horse riding, or fishing.

Apartment Recommendations

Below are some of the best apartment recommendations in Kefalonia:

Polymnia I-Top Floor Apartment: This is a spacious and elegant apartment that is located near Lourdas Beach. It has 2 bedrooms, 1 bathroom, a living room, a kitchen, and a balcony with sea views. It can accommodate up to 5 guests. The apartment also offers free Wi-Fi, free parking, air conditioning, and a TV. You can enjoy the shared garden and barbecue facilities. The apartment is close to many restaurants, bars, shops, and attractions.

By the Beach–Apt.1 (Studio) Kefalonia: This is a cosy and modern studio that is located right on the beach of Karavomylos village. It has 1 bedroom, 1 bathroom, a kitchenette, and a patio with sea views. It can accommodate up to 4 guests. The studio also offers free Wi-Fi, free parking, air conditioning, and a TV. You can enjoy the shared pool and garden. The studio is close to Melissani Cave and Sami town.

Zoe beachfront apartment Karavomylos: This is a luxurious and stylish apartment that is located on the beachfront of Karavomylos village. It has 3 bedrooms, 2 bathrooms, a living room, a kitchen, and a balcony with sea views. It can accommodate up to 6 guests. The apartment also offers free Wi-Fi, free parking, air conditioning, and a TV. You can enjoy the private garden and barbecue facilities. The apartment is close to Melissani Cave and Sami town.

Nerissa Bungalows No.4 Independent, near the beach: This is a charming and comfortable bungalow that is located near Skala Beach. It has 2 bedrooms, 1 bathroom, a living room, a kitchen, and a terrace with garden views. It can accommodate up to 5 guests. The bungalow also offers free Wi-Fi, free parking, air conditioning, and a TV. You can enjoy the shared pool and garden. The bungalow is close to many restaurants, bars, shops, and attractions.

Tzivras Studio Apartment: This is a bright and cosy studio that is located near Argostoli town. It has 1 bedroom, 1 bathroom, a kitchenette, and a balcony with mountain views. It can accommodate up to 2 guests. The studio also offers free Wi-Fi, free parking, air conditioning, and a TV. You can enjoy the shared pool and garden. The studio is close to many attractions, such as the Archaeological Museum, the Korgialenio Historical and Folklore Museum, and the De Bosset Bridge.

Conclusion

Kefalonia is a beautiful Greek island that offers many attractions and activities for visitors who want to enjoy a relaxing and memorable holiday. Whether you are looking for stunning beaches, fascinating caves, charming villages, or adventurous activities, you will find something to enjoy on this island. You can also learn more about the history, culture, and cuisine of Kefalonia by visiting some of its historical and cultural attractions, such as the Venetian castle in Assos, the Archaeological Museum in Argostoli, the Korgialenio Historical and Folklore Museum in Argostoli, and the Monastery of Agios Gerasimos. You can also taste some of the traditional dishes of Kefalonia, such as the Kefalonian meat pie, the cod pie, the rabbit stifado, and the aliada.

Kefalonia is also a destination that cares about the environment and the sustainability of its tourism. You can find many eco-friendly accommodation and transportation options on the island, such as White Rocks Hotel Kefalonia, Hotel Summery, Mounda Beach Hotel, Studios Diamanto, public buses, ferry, walking or cycling . You can also join some ethical experiences and wildlife conservation projects on the island, such as Wildlife Sense, Katelios Group, Kefalonia Tours, and Sugaro pastry shop.

Kefalonia is a wonderful destination for travelers who want to enjoy the beauty and culture of Greece without spending too much money. There are many budget-friendly accommodation and food options on the island, such as Lassi Hotel, Hotel Oceanis, Taverna Patsouras, Steki Grill, Tsobos Garden Grillhouse, and Sugaro pastry shop. You can also visit some of the free and affordable attractions on the island, such as Myrtos Beach, Melissani Cave, Assos village and castle, Mount Ainos National Park, and Argostoli Harbour.

Kefalonia is a paradise for families with children, as it offers many attractions and activities that are suitable for all ages. You can find many child-friendly accommodation and facilities on the island, such as Emelisse Nature Resort, Hotel Summery, Mounda Beach Hotel, Studios Diamanto, kids pool, playground, game room, and babysitting. You can also enjoy some fun and educational attractions and activities on the island, such as Melissani Cave, Dias Beekeeping, turtle spotting tour or monk seal tour by Kefalonia Tours, or Sugaro pastry shop.

Kefalonia is a perfect destination for couples who want to enjoy a romantic and relaxing holiday. You can find many luxury resorts and facilities on the island, such as F Zeen resort, White Rocks Hotel Kefalonia resort, Ionian Emerald Resort resort, spa treatments, wine tasting, or sailing. You can also enjoy some of the most beautiful and secluded spots on the island, such as Petani Beach, Antisamos Beach, Emplisi Beach, or Assos village and castle.

Kefalonia is an island that has something for everyone. It is a place where you can enjoy nature, culture, cuisine, adventure, relaxation, romance, or family fun. It is an island that will make you fall in love with Greece. It is an island that you will never forget. I hope you enjoyed this travel guide and found it helpful. I hope you have a wonderful time on this beautiful island!

Manufactured by Amazon.ca
Acheson, AB